Get Out of the Rut *and on with* Your Life

Second Edition

Praise for
Get Out of the Rut and On With Your Life

Deb Erickson's book is a must-read for anyone who wants the inside scoop on how to succeed in these challenging times. With humor and self disclosure she offers a one on one intimate coaching session that leads the reader to greater levels of engagement in life, providing the solutions that guide gently and powerfully to the achievement of Ones› true potential.

— Sedena C. Cappannelli, Co-founder of AgeNation

"Get Out of the Rut and on with YOUR LIFE" is a powerful tool for success. My 35-year career in collegiate athletics has given me an inside glimpse at some incredible coaches and motivators. Deb is the one they go to for their inspiration!

— Konn Apostol, Portland, OR

Deb Erickson is a GIFT. Her book speaks to the heart, mind and spirit. Your heart will be full, your mind will be set to conquer anything you have ever dreamed of experiencing, and your spirit will soar.

— Charlotte A. Whitfield, El Paso, TX

Nothing can change until YOU do. Deb teaches you step by step how to delete the old files in your brain and start to develop new habits. This book is changing lives – It changed mine.

— Annie O'Connell, Albuquerque, NM

Deb Erickson helped me identify my strengths and make them productive. I've learned to "clean out" my mental files and to focus on forward thinking and positive action. Don't just read her book – do the work for a lifetime of results!

— Marcia Lohner, Detroit, MI

Deb is the best! She is intuitive, knowledgeable and inspiring. I have read many motivational books and listened to lots of CDs but none have impacted my life the way Deb has. In three short months I have changed my life. I have learned how to bring the best parts of me to the surface. I'm on my way.

— Lovey Frazier, Albuquerque, NM

You've heard a picture paints a thousand words. Deb's words paint a thousand pictures in your mind to empower you to artistically create the most beautiful life God intended for you to live! She is a HUGE blessing in my life.

— Marilyn Schmucker, Bloomington, IL

Get Out of the Rut *and on with* Your Life

Second Edition

Published and distributed in the United States of America by:
ICAN Institute, Inc. www.deberickson.com

The author of this book does not dispense medical advice or prescribe the use of any techniques as a form of treatment for physical, emotional, or medical problems without the advice of a physician, either directly or indirectly. The intent of the author is only to offer information of a general nature to help you in your quest for emotional wellbeing. In the event you use any of the information in this book for yourself, which is your constitutional right, the author and publisher assume no responsibility for your actions.

Editor: First Edition – Mary Erickson
Editors: Second Edition – Jana Henton and Marilyn Moyer

Cover Design: Sara Khoudary

ISBN 978-0-615-18281-0

Limited First Edition, December 2007
Limited Second Edition, January 2013

Printed in the United States of America

Dedication

This book is lovingly dedicated to all those who throughout my life have contributed to who I am today.

To my teachers, counselors, coaches, mentors, and friends, I appreciate you more than you will ever know. You have enriched my life, inspired me to reach for the stars, guided my steps, given me opportunities to grow, and taught me to listen to my own inner guidance. A special thank you to Grandpa Erickson, Chris Voelz, Becky Bosch, Melinda Balling, and Esther & Jerry Hicks.

Thank you to my parents, who for more than 50 years have believed in my potential and supported me in pursuing my dreams. You gave me the strength and freedom to find my own way. Thank you for loving and accepting me without reservation.

To my editors - Mom, without you the first edition would not have been possible. Thank you, for your unique genius and eternal generosity. To Jana Henton and Marilyn Moyer, for helping me bring this second edition to life. Thank you for your technical expertise, constant encouragement, and endless patience.

To those with whom I have the greatest honor of all, sharing our lives together - Nolan, for your passion and competitive intensity, Collin, for your determination and tenacious focus, Krista, for your sweet inspiration, and Jana, for your unconditional love. You have each touched my life with your special gifts. You bring me more joy than I can possibly express.

Table of Contents

Introduction

This revised 2nd edition contains much of the original transcript of *Get Out of the Rut and On With Your Life*. After five years of coaching thousands of women past their ruts, I realized I needed to share more of the tools, success stories, and new neuroscience techniques that have been met with great success. I have developed some new processes to increase awareness of the limiting mechanisms of the mind as well as transformational tools to consciously reprogram your success set point. I have included an additional chapter of new material for you. You will find enlightening new stories, powerful new mind mastering techniques, and inspirational insights to help you bust through your current ruts and step into your personal greatness.

I have spent the last 20 years speaking to hundreds of thousands of people about the power and pitfalls of the mind. If you have been to one of my workshops, seminars, or stage performances, you know that I love what I do. It makes sense because my father was a pastor and administrator; my mother, a drama and speech teacher, as well as my first basketball coach. I guess it's a bit of a no-brainer that I would be a teacher and that I love the stage.

I like calling what I do "edutainment," because I love to teach and entertain at the same time. I learned a long time ago that words don't teach, but experiences can. I know that if I can help you laugh, you can let go of the stranglehold that your limiting beliefs have on your life. I know that if I can give you a personal, physical, real-life experience, then you will take home with you a touchstone that can be the foundation upon which you can build a new reality.

That is why I love to finish my programs with a board-break. It's a great metaphor to help my participants experience a personal "breakthrough" in their lives.

How I Help

Not long ago, I had a woman come to an event and tell me that she still has the board she broke with me more than a decade ago. She told me that breaking that board changed her life because it was the first time she had the courage to take a risk. In just ten years she went from a single mom on welfare, with no education, to a college graduate who is now halfway through her master's degree and owns her own business. She has a six-figure income and is putting her two kids through college as well. WOW!

She told me that her broken board has been her only trophy in life. She keeps it on her dresser so that every morning she can remember the thrill of breaking through the self-doubt that had limited her life. She tried to give me the credit, but I reminded her that all I did was hold the board. I may have inspired her to believe in herself, but the true greatness she had discovered was within her all along.

Why I Wrote This Book

That's when I knew I wanted to take my program to the next level and write this book. It's an opportunity for me to be your life coach wherever you are.

Just like my stage programs, this book is full of my own stories and life lessons from 50 years—rich in both failures and successes. I've included experiences and insights I've gained throughout 20 years on the road as a speaker, entertainer, and trainer, as well as 10 years as an educator and coach. The truth is that it is a synthesis of all that I have lived, all that I have taught, and all that I have learned from the real-life mentors, coaches, and teachers with whom I have studied.

What I want you to know is that I am walking this same path with you. The activities I will give you are the same ones I have done and still do myself. I am including many exercises that I have found make the greatest impact on the lives of the people I have had the honor to work with over the years. I have put the best of the best into this book for you.

Chapter 1

Getting Started

My Awakening

Back peddling as fast as I could, I watched as the basketball flew back to my side of the court. In a heartbeat I was standing toe-to-toe with a tall, power forward who sized-up my short stature and decided that she was going to blow by me. One look into her eyes and I knew I was in trouble.

She faked to my right and, just like always, I fell for it. All it took was one quick crossover dribble and she was passing right by me. My old patterns took over and I did what I had done a million times before, I reached for the ball. The instant the whistle blew, I knew I had gotten caught. It was the biggest game of my high school career and I had fouled out.

My eyes filled with tears as I hung my head and shuffled over to the bench. I looked up for just a moment into my coach's eyes and saw her disappointment. "Move your feet, Erickson," she said, "I've told you a hundred times. You know better than to reach." I did know better but when things got tough, I fell back into my old habits.

When I got honest with myself, I had to admit that my game was in a rut. I had gotten lazy and developed some bad habits. Sure, I had enough raw talent to play at this level, but if I wanted to take my game to the next level, I'd have to kick it up a notch and make some real changes. Sitting on the bench that night while my team finished the game without me was a real wake-up call.

Your Wake-Up Call

Where do you find yourself at this moment in your life?

- Are you truly happy, or have you gotten into an emotional rut?
- Do you find it easy to change, or are you stuck in some bad habits?
- Are you the master of your own mind, or do you indulge in negative thinking like worry and doubt?
- Are you living the life of your dreams or have you settled for something less?
- Do you wake up each day excited about the adventure that lies ahead, or are you on automatic pilot barely making it though the day?

Changing Patterns

If you find yourself repeating the same patterns over and over again even though you really want to move in a new direction, then this book is for you. I must warn you, in order to get out of the rut you must DO something different. I'm sure you have heard the definition of insanity: "Insanity is doing the same thing over and over and expecting different results."

Well, it's time to stop the insanity and ***Get Out of the Rut and On With Your Life.*** If you want different results than you are currently getting, something has to change. You must focus on different thoughts, reach for different feelings, adopt different beliefs, take different actions, experiment with different strategies, test-out different philosophies, make different choices, and embrace different expectations. To get something different, you must **become** someone different.

I've been blessed with amazing teachers, coaches, and role models throughout my life. One thing all taught me is that life is an endless journey. Each new day, I have a choice. I can try something different, or I can stay in my comfortable routine. I can reach for more, or I can retreat to the safety of my habitual patterns. I can risk change, or I can stick to the mental and emotional ruts I have become accustomed to. If I choose to stay where I am, I can count on getting more of what I've already got. If I want something greater, something different, then I must change something.

My Role as Coach

Let me be for you what my mentors have been for me. Let me inspire you to reach for more and then give you the tools you need to get there.

- I'll tell you real life stories that will give you examples of both successes and failures.
- I'll help you explore your life history so you can discover what thoughts and beliefs have brought you to this particular place and time.
- I'll offer you a new way to view your mind and provide the tools you need to shift the neuro-programming that has caused you to fail in the past.
- I'll give you drills to help you practice new patterns to make the changes you desire.
- I'll demonstrate how to celebrate your successes and learn from your setbacks.
- I'll walk with you as you choose to change.

> *Progress is impossible without change,*
> *and those who cannot change their minds*
> *cannot change anything.*
>
> George Bernard Shaw

Your Role as Student

The big question for you is this: What do you want from this process? Every page of this book has potential magic on it. The activities have the power to transform your life.

If I am going to play the role of your coach, there are a few things I need from you.

#1. Stay open-minded.

It's possible that one of your old patterns is to discount new ideas. Remember, in order to change, you may need to challenge some of your old ideas and accept some new ones.

#2. Be a student.

Test it out, try it on, and listen to that small voice inside. Don't take anything I say as the gospel truth. It is true that if you seek, you will find—but you must be a seeker.

#3. Commit to taking your "game" to the next level.

I will challenge your thinking and push your buttons. That's what coaches do. But if you really want to get out of your rut, I need you to give me everything you've got.

If you are willing to do the work and make the changes, it is possible for you to live the life you were born to live.

What to Expect

If you come to this book with an expectation that it holds the keys to finding what you are seeking, then you will find them. Not because I am so amazing, but because you are. So let's get clear about what you want right now. Check every statement that you agree with and add anything you want that is not on this list.

Ask yourself this question: When I finish reading this book and participating in all the activities, what do I want to happen in my life?

I want to:

- Liberate my full potential
- Eliminate doubt and judgment
- Break through oppressive mental limits
- Free my spirit
- Discover my passion and purpose in life
- Feel more confident and be more decisive
- Experience more joy on a daily basis
- Live life from a more optimistic vantage point
- Adopt an abundant mentality
- Become more self-empowered
- Find my place of peace
- Live my bliss
- Lighten up and have more fun

Great! You can do all that and more if you can come to this process with an open mind and heart.

What's the Process?

Please do NOT get hooked on semantics. Life is full of variety, and I want to honor that diversity by using as many ways as possible to describe something so that no matter what your heritage, cultural conditioning, religious beliefs, gender, personality traits, or age may be, you will be able to find something that helps you feel comfortable with this material.

Try not to label and categorize your experiences as you move through this process. Take what you want, and leave the rest behind. Trust yourself. Nothing has to be rushed; nothing needs to be forced. Everything can unfold in a gentle, graceful, and lighthearted manner.

The activities and exercises are designed to walk you through a very specific process. Each one builds on the one before. You can jump in anywhere you like, but you will gain the most benefit if you follow the steps and allow your mind to grow comfortable with each new concept and discovery before you proceed to the next one. Some activities may take more time than you can devote to them in one sitting; no problem, just come back to them over and over until you are ready to move on.

This material is presented in a style suggesting that this book is a hybrid. It's true; I couldn't decide whether to write an inspirational, feel-good storybook, or a how-to, self-help manual, or a seminar-style workbook. So you get all three. I have no idea what to call it, but this I do know, you will only get out of this book what you put into it. If you use it as light bedtime reading, you will enjoy the humor, be entertained by the stories, and be inspired by the life lessons. If you are looking to make real life changes, then you must commit to being a student of this material.

How to Prepare

My suggestion is that you get some supplies before we begin. If you are going to be a student, then you need to act like one. You are going to have assignments, and yes, even pop quizzes. Okay, maybe there won't be any pop quizzes, but in a way, isn't living life every day like a pop quiz? Each day you can put these new ideas to the test.

Treat this book like a college textbook. Underline things that are important to you. Write in the margins and fill in the blanks. This book is like a coach's playbook for us to work through together.

Your project supplies should include a highlighter, colored pens, glue stick, scissors, and most importantly a 3 ring binder. Create some tabs so you can find your notes and activities easily. You can label the tabs as follows:

Thoughts and Impressions
Activities
Joy Journal
This Stuff Works
Self-Talk

You will need a place to truly capture the changes you are going through. This notebook is the place where you will record your discoveries and do your assignments as we work through this material together. I'll give you more details as we move through each chapter, but for now, here are a few suggestions about each of the tabs.

Thoughts and Impressions: This is where you can write anything and everything you are thinking about as we progress. It's also a great place for you to record your notes from other books on the same topics.

Activities

Here you can record the activities and assignments
I give you in each chapter.

Joy Journal

In this segment, write about something each day that brings you joy. Every day, ask yourself these questions:

What am I happy about?

What do I have to be grateful for?

What do I appreciate?

Take a few moments each day to write down all the things that make you smile, warm your heart, bring you peace, and make your life worth living. You will soon discover that the more you focus on the things in your life that you appreciate, the more you will see desirable things show up. This one tool will revolutionize your life.

This *Stuff* Works: This is what I call your evidence journal. Record everything that happens to you that is a match to what you are learning. Later you can go back and review all the REAL evidence you are discovering and find that this stuff really does work.

Self-Talk: Some people would call this segment Affirmations. You can call it whatever you want, but this is a place where you can record positive mental pictures and verbal statements that affirm your greatness.

I'll give you some ideas of things you can write in your notebook. You pick the ones that are right for you. When we are done, you will have pages and pages of new self-talk that support you and the changes you wish to make in your life.

Are you ready to get started?

Okay then, let's get you

Out of the Rut and On With Your Life!

We tend to get what we expect.
Norman Vincent Peale

Take the IQ test

Ever wonder if you have what it takes to live the life of your dreams? It is so easy to look at others who have accomplished what you want to accomplish and say, "Well I'm no Susie, I can't possibly do what she did." The truth is you have EVERYTHING you need to achieve your dreams. It's not about finding something you need; it's about acknowledging you have it and then knowing how to use it.

I've devised a short RutBusting IQ test to see where your personal awareness and tools currently lie. Take a minute to go online and take the test. It only takes three minutes, but the information you receive will be profound. Go to: **www.deberickson.com**, and click on the link to take the IQ Test.

Chapter 2

The Power and Pitfalls of the Mind

Over the years, my curiosity has caused me to read and research a wide range of scientific studies and new theories about the power of the mind. Much of the recent neuro-science research suggests that our minds process information in pictures and appear to be stimulated by color and images more than by language.

As a teacher, I know the power of stories and visual metaphors. I have spent much of my adult life finding ways to communicate with my clients about the powers and pitfalls of the human mind. My hope has always been that a better understanding would lead to simple tools and techniques to support others in making the changes in their lives they longed for but didn't believe possible.

While any metaphor is not an exact replica of the actual workings of the brain, it does help most people to create a visual image to grasp concepts in a new way. So, for the sake of our discussion in this book, I'm going to compare the mind to a computer.

Brain Versus Computer

Picture for a minute that you are sitting at your desk in front of your computer screen. What does it look like? Does your desktop have small icons and file folders running down the side of the screen? Now imagine that you click on one of those files. What happens? It opens up, right?

Now here is the question: What's in that file? Most people say, "My *stuff*." But it is more than that. Some of it is your boss's *stuff*, or

Microsoft's *stuff*, or even downloaded information. Much like your computer, your brain holds information from many sources.

The truth is that anyone who has had access to you has been giving you stuff that you have been dropping into your mental files your entire life. Every life experience has been noted, labeled, sorted, and filed. You have been sticking *stuff* into your files every minute, 24/7.

Here's how it works. When you have a physical experience, no matter what it is, your five senses evaluate that experience and then send messages to your body. Your mind must evaluate those messages to determine if any action is required. Basically it searches the hard drive for information so that it knows exactly what to do. It wants to answer several questions: What is this? Is this important? Do I need to do something about it? Your brain sifts and sorts to determine if an experience is critical for your survival.

Fire Burns

Here's an example. Imagine that you're only two years old and you are at your first cookout. Left unattended, you wander over to the bonfire that has burned down to red-hot coals. Intrigued by the beautiful colors, you reach down to touch the glowing coals. In the instant you touch the coals, your senses send pain messages to your brain and your brain sends action impulses back to your hand that cause you to recoil. Your mind immediately adds this new experience to the survival programming of your hard drive. *Fire burns!* Then it creates a file and stores this experience in that file. The pain you feel is your physical evidence that your belief is true—fire burns.

The more experiences you have, stories you hear, or pictures you see, the deeper ingrained this new belief becomes. Your brain now accepts it as absolute Fact. This new belief will now guide your future behavior. Once a belief is created, the mind will continuously search for evidence to confirm and strengthen that belief. It will actually ignore anything that contradicts this new belief as unimportant or false information. In other words, it only acknowledges information that matches or confirms the programming it currently holds.

The next time you are near fire, all kinds of warning bells and whistles begin to go off inside your brain stem as previous files are accessed in order to prevent you from getting hurt again. The brain stem actually contains a primitive warning system that helped us survive our "cave days". While it is perfectly designed for true threats to survival, it often is triggered by the slightest little incident, releasing stress hormones into our bodies. When that happens, conscious thought is lost and the brain throws us into crisis mode. All too often, our minds make erroneous conclusions and we are left with mislabeled files, unfounded fears and faulty beliefs that can control our lives.

Your Curious Mind

The conscious mind always wants an answer. It can't stand not knowing, so when it searches the hard drive and can't find a suitable answer, it will fabricate an answer. That's right. It just MAKES STUFF UP! Call it analyzing, evaluating, extrapolating, or even hypothesizing. It doesn't matter how fancy the term is, it is basically only guessing. Here is where the real problem begins. When the mind tries to fill the void by coming up with an answer, it doesn't know that it just pulled that answer out of thin air. It grasps on to that illusion and calls it FACT. Once your brain does that, it is committed to that FALSE FACT for life. That FALSE FACT becomes a belief.

When you have a life experience, the mind always wants to evaluate that experience. The mind always asks, "Why? Why did this happen to me?" If it was something good, the mind wants to know why so it can repeat the experience to bring you more joy. If it was bad, the brain is determined to protect you from ever experiencing that pain again. In order to protect you, it MUST have an answer to the question, "WHY?"

Limited Understanding

Think back to early man. When the ground shook and the lava flowed out of the mountain, people died. When the holy men of the tribe asked the question, "Why has this happened to our people?" their brains gave them the answer. "The Mountain Gods are unhappy."

Of course, their next question was, "How do we keep this pain from happening again?" Somewhere along the road, the idea popped into someone's mind that if they sacrificed several virgins every full moon, the Mountain Gods would never get angry again.

Primitive men didn't have the scientific understanding to know that tectonic plates shift. That simple knowledge could have saved a lot of virgins.

But honestly, we are almost as unsophisticated today as they were hundreds of years ago. Our brains still ask why and still make up answers. Yes, we have come a long way, but you need to accept the truth that today our beliefs—like those of early man—are based on the current limitations of our scientific and cultural understanding. Like early man, we are still making *stuff* up. We may not be sacrificing virgins anymore, but instead we sacrifice our potential. When the brain makes up reasons to explain why we can't do or be or have something we want, we are literally throwing our hopes and dreams into the volcano.

Programming the Mind

Let's get back to our discussion about the hard drive of your mind. When you were born, you came into this world wired and ready. Part of that wiring is your personality type, processing and learning styles, basic survival instincts, and personal drives. However, most of your mental programming is installed little by little through life experiences. The vast majority of that programming happens before the age of seven.

Most of this programming comes from the caretakers who raised and influenced us. This social programming teaches us what our culture believes is right and what's wrong. It teaches us our society's expectations of the roles we should play. It also sets the limits and boundaries of what is considered possible.

This social blueprint is based on several criteria: your gender, race, religion, culture, the social and economic status of your family, the beliefs and behaviors of your caretakers, as well as the philosophy of those who have power or influence over you. Much of who you are today was programmed into you during those all-important, formative years when your brain was downloading and accepting without question the beliefs of others and then making those beliefs your own.

This programming basically becomes your mind's operating system through which all your life experiences are filtered, defined, and filed. When you have an experience, your mind wants to label and categorize it. But imagine what might happen if the file is mislabeled or misinterpreted. What if decisions are based on faulty or outdated information? When that happens, your life can be limited based on files that contain false assumptions and faulty information. That means that you are interpreting the world through flawed filters. Your view of yourself and your world is based on this programming. The big question is what happens when the programming is flawed?

Negative Singing File

Let's take a look at the files and how they work together. Let's open a file and see what you have in it. Open your file called *singing.* What's in that file? It literally contains memories of every experience you've ever had related to singing. So if those are great memories, then the file is full of good information. But if you've had some bad experiences, then your file will probably be coded with a BIG warning sign.

Perhaps it has these letters written in Big Bold type: **I CAN'T SING.** Inside you will find all the negative experiences you need to prove that this statement is true. But let's take a look for a minute at how that belief got created.

Maybe, when you were in second grade, you had a negative experience during music class. What if your teacher asked you to sing, and when you did, horrible noises came out of your mouth? What happened? Your second-grade classmates probably laughed and pointed and teased you relentlessly. Why? Because that is what second graders do. But your little second-grade mind would not have understood that. Your little second-grade mind would immediately jump to the conclusion that you can't sing and that you should never try again. One experience—only one experience—and that file is labeled forever unless you intentionally go back in and rewrite it. Once a belief is accepted, it is rarely questioned; therefore, the mind will desperately hold onto it as FACT.

Linking Files

Now the brain does something truly amazing at this point. It begins to link files and emotions together. Not only will the brain say, "I can't sing," but it will connect other files using a hot link much like internet sites do. When one file is opened, all other linked files are also opened.

Let's go back to that fateful day in music class. Perhaps you decided that you would never volunteer again. Or maybe you decided that if you can't sing, then maybe you can't speak in public either. Or maybe you decided that your teacher was intentionally picking on you because of your race or gender.

What's really amazing is that all those connected files carry the same emotion and energy of the first. That's why it's so tough to figure out where some of your fears and beliefs come from. The brain links experiences that happened in close proximity.

Here's another example. If you are feeling the emotional pain of a relationship that broke up at the same time that you heard a love song or smelled a certain fragrance, then that song and fragrance will be linked to the emotional pain. That's why sometimes you have an emotional reaction to an experience you can't explain. The brain is responding to an old link—an old connection that may no longer be serving you.

Rewriting Your Files

The good news is that you have total control over your mental files. You can go back and rewrite and reconnect the files of your choosing. Here are a few things you need to know in order to begin the process.

 # 1. Files can't be deleted.

Sorry, although it would be cool if you could just drag a file to the trash or recycle bin like you can on your computer, the brain doesn't work that way. This is because the mind doesn't understand negative commands. If I say, "Don't think of a pink elephant," what does your mind do? It ignores the word *don't* and goes in search of a picture of a pink elephant. If you have actually seen a pink elephant, it will access your memories and open that file. If not, no problem! It will just make one up using your imagination. Remember, your mind is powerful; it will give you whatever you ask for.

 # 2. Open files become active.

Once a file is opened, just like on your desktop, it becomes "active." If you think to yourself, "I'm in debt and I need to get out of debt," guess what file gets opened? Right, DEBT! You can't create financial freedom when your debt file is open and active.

If your mother says to you, "Don't spill your milk," guess what you will do. Yep, you will spill it just about every time. The suggestion "Don't spill" causes your mind to search, open, and focus on the command: Spill. Whatever you focus on, you will get more of the same. That's how the brain works.

 # 3. The mind never shuts down.

The mind is constantly in motion. The big question is, what are you thinking right now? Some research says that women's minds think about 85,000 thoughts a day, and men's about 65,000 thoughts a day. Although your mind can think many thoughts in rapid succession, it can only focus on one thought at a time.

Researchers also tell us that nearly 85 percent of the thoughts you think today are the same ones you thought yesterday.

That means that there's not a lot of original thinking going on. It's like you have a little cassette recorder in your mind. Every day you wake up and rewind the tape back to the beginning, and through the day it plays all of the old messages that you have been collecting throughout your life. Then, every so often, you add a bit of new or original thought to that tape. But most of what goes on in your head is the same stuff that's been running through it for years. We call that your mental chatter. Since you have patterns of thought that constantly run through your mind, the important question is this: Is your mental chatter positive—full of optimism and opportunity? Or is it negative—full of limiting thoughts and painful memories?

Activity 1

Past Files

If you have areas in your life that you're not happy with, chances are you have information in your files that's keeping you from having what you want. A good way to see what is in those files is to open them up and dump the contents onto the floor and see what's in there. That way, if there is something there that you don't like, you can change it. I know this sounds like a no-brainer, but I need to say it anyway. You can't change it if you don't know it's there.

Go to your notebook and in the section you labeled "Activities" do the following. Pick a mental file and write the name of that file at the top of your page. Here's a popular one we can do together.

Let's open your file on *money*. Now write down everything that's in your file. Write down every thought you have about it, positive or negative. Think about all the mental chatter that runs through your mind—things your parents told you, things you've read, things you say to your peers in the lunchroom, things you see on CNN.

What do you think when you look at your bank balance? What do you say to yourself when the bills come due? What are the subtle messages you hear in your mind when you are window-shopping? What are the thoughts that run through your head when you are planning the family vacation or facing another Christmas? Write them all down. Don't question them now; just get them down on paper.

Here is an example of a list that a woman in one of my workshops wrote. If any of her messages work for you, leave them in but cross out those that aren't a match for you.

- There's never enough.
- There is no free lunch.
- Money just goes through my fingers.
- Money is the root of all evil.
- I can't afford that.
- Money doesn't grow on trees.
- You got to work hard for the money.
- I'm always broke.
- Rich people are wasteful.
- I can never get ahead.
- I'll never get out of debt.
- The economy stinks.
- I have barely enough to get by.
- It's the government's fault.

Sometimes the messages we get from our early programming are more subtle, but the beliefs are every bit as strong.

Examples: Tom and Molly

I have a client—I'll call him Tom—whose parents were divorced when he was in junior high school. Every time Tom asked his dad for something, he would get a huge sob story. His dad would sigh and say, "Do you really have to have that? I have to give your mother all my money in child support, and I can barely pay the mortgage payment." Those statements laid some serious guilt upon his son and left a very strong message to NOT ask for anything. Tom would constantly talk about how his poor dad never had enough money. He laid awake at night worrying about whether they would have to move if his dad couldn't make the house payments. The truth about his father was far from the helpless victim he portrayed himself to be, but to a young boy, the negative messages were deeply implanted.

I had another client—I'll call her Molly—who lived with her dad after her mother's death. Her dad was a door-to-door salesman who was always on the road. Molly traveled with him, living in a second-hand camper. Her father home schooled her on the back roads of America. She recounts those memories with fondness. They always seemed to have enough and her life felt like an endless string of adventures. When they wanted something, they would go out and sell more cleaning products. Her dad always told her that the world was her oyster and that whatever she wanted was just around the corner, only three doors away. That was because he knew the statistics—that every three doors they knocked on would land him a sale.

In truth, Molly's dad had a fraction of the actual dollars that Tom's dad had. Molly's dad was a traveling salesman who never owned a home. He had an eighth grade education, but he gave to Molly a wealthy mindset. She had a money file that gave her the foundation to become a millionaire as a pharmaceutical sales representative. She still believes that the next sale is just three calls away.

Tom's dad, a college graduate, was a teacher. He had plenty of money, but he passed on a belief in lack to Tom who still to this day struggles to make ends meet every month. The difference is not their education or their family's financial inheritance; the difference is their beliefs about money. Molly expected prosperity; Tom expected poverty. They both got exactly what they believed they would get.

Lifestyle

Part 1 — Now take a few moments and write out your own personal story that has impacted your money file. What are your personal life events or stories that have shaped your beliefs about money?

Part 2 — Once you have written out your story, go back and review it for money themes that you picked up from your life experiences. How did you interpret these events? What decisions did you make about money, debt, abundance, and lack? Go back to your previous file activity sheet and write these additional beliefs on your list.

Here is what Molly and Tom wrote in their life stories:

Molly: The world is my playground.
Selling is the greatest profession in the world.
My income potential is unlimited.

Tom: People are always after what little money I have.
I can hardly make enough to pay the rent.
I can never get ahead.

Limiting or Empowering Thoughts

Part 1 — Now I want you to go back through the list of thoughts that are in your money file, one by one, and ask yourself this question: Does this thought limit me or empower me? If it is a thought or belief that limits your potential or makes you feel a negative emotion, put a minus sign in front of it. If thinking this thought or belief empowers you or makes you feel positive emotion, put a plus sign in front of it.

Don't get caught up in whether you think it is true or not, just ask yourself these questions:

- Does believing or thinking this thought support me in what I want for my life?
- Does this thought move me closer to my dreams or further away from them?
- Does this thought fill me with fear, or does it make me feel confident?
- Does this thought make me feel hopeless or hopeful?
- Does this thought make me feel powerless or powerful?

Part 2 — Let's do a little simple math. Give yourself one point for each of your empowering beliefs/thoughts, and subtract one for each of the limiting ones.

How did you do? Do you invest your mental energy thinking positive and empowering thoughts, or do you wallow in negativity? You can see that if you spend the vast majority of your time thinking and believing in lack, you're going to really struggle creating wealth. It is a great activity to help you identify where you spend the majority of your mental time.

Some people say to me, "But, Deb, you don't understand my situation. In my case, you have to understand it really is true." To that comment I always respond, "The more you argue for your lack and limitations, the stronger bond you build with them and the more you guarantee their continued presence in your life." Even if you have an enormous amount of evidence to prove that your belief is Fact, holding that belief deprives or robs you of power, authority, and influence.

My *Spelling* File

Let me tell you a personal story to illustrate my point. When I was a kid, everybody told me I was a lousy speller. My report cards said so, "Debbie is a poor speller." During spelling bees I stood in line at the front of the room scared to death, waiting for my turn. I knew that when Mrs. Morgan gave me my word, my mind would go blank and I would misspell the word. I just knew I would be the first one to miss a word and have to sit down. I knew it because it had happened every time we had a spelling bee.

One day, Mrs. Morgan was feeling sorry for me so when it came to me she said, "Debbie, I'm going to give you an easy word. Your word is I, as in 'I am happy.'" As always, the pressure built inside my head, the room started to sway, and I could hear the laughter of my classmates as I messed up the easiest word on the list. I couldn't think. The message, "Debbie is a poor speller. Debbie is a poor speller" swirled around inside my head. I couldn't even think of possible letters that I might use. So I gave up without even venturing a guess. I got out of the line and returned to my seat. In effect, I opened that file on spelling and deposited the memory of the most humiliating day of my young life. I knew for a Fact that I could not spell! But, it didn't stop there. My mind started to link files like crazy. I decided that I was stupid. That I couldn't read, write, or do arithmetic. I decided that when it came to learning, I was a complete loser.

With those beliefs, you can imagine how I struggled throughout my entire educational career. I had such a low SAT score that no college would take me. But I had a dream of being a PE teacher and I knew I needed a degree to fulfill that dream. I found a state college that had a "special" program for kids like me—kids with lots of personality and promise but poor test scores. After giving me several aptitude tests, the college instructors finally discovered I was dyslexic.

The dictionary says that dyslexia is "a learning disorder marked by a severe difficulty in recognizing and understanding written language, leading to spelling and writing problems." So there you have it. The good news is that dyslexia is not caused by low intelligence or brain damage. I wish I had known that when I was seven years old.

On With My Story

When I look at that belief—I can't spell—it feels Very true. I have hundreds of life experiences that verify the validity of that belief and even a label proven with test scores. You can't get more real than that. But I still have to ask myself, is that belief limiting or empowering me? Does this belief serve and support me, or does it set me up for failure?

The answer is obvious; the thoughts that I am a poor speller and just plain stupid were very disempowering. That thought created a mental block that I could not get past until someone came along and said, "Lots of people are dyslexic, Deb. It's no big deal. All you need to do is learn a different reading system, use the spell check on your computer, and hire an accountant to do the math." That one statement freed me. It gave me hope and released the death grip of my belief that because I couldn't spell, I was a loser.

I graduated from Illinois State University with a 3.5 GPA and a degree in education. I've completed over 20 hours of master's level coursework with a perfect 4.0. I am still "spelling challenged," but my new belief about spelling is that it really doesn't matter. I have great people around me who take care of my spelling needs. I am free to share my gifts and talents with the world without that limiting thought weighing me down.

Activity 4

Your Life Files

Part 1 — It's time for you to look at your life files and see what thoughts are holding you back. Use your notebook and write these file headings at the top of the page. Leave a whole page for each file. Take your time and find out what thoughts and beliefs you have in these files.

- My job/career
- My body/health
- My love life/relationships
- My family
- My finances

Part 2 — After you get the thoughts listed, go back through and put a plus for the positive statements or minus for the negative ones. Let's see where you spend the majority of your thinking power on each of these topics.

In a later chapter, we will spend some time talking about how to change or rewrite the negative or limiting thoughts but, for now, it's important to get them all down on paper.

> *Our brains become magnetized with the vibrations of our thoughts and mental images. These magnets attract to us the forces, the people, the circumstances of life which harmonize with the nature of our dominating vibration.*
>
> Napoleon Hill

Chapter 3

Upgrade Your Operating System

The mind holds as absolute anything that it has been programmed to believe. If you doubt this, just look at history. Even when science has confirmed new knowledge of how our world works, the mind can't let go of previous beliefs. That's why new ideas and discoveries often require hundreds of years to be accepted. Often, several generations have to come and go, each new generation growing up with less resistance to the new idea, until it is accepted as FACT—as reality.

A finite mind can't comprehend a concept of infinite. If you review human history, you will see that when we, as a society, decide something is FACT, we will ignore any evidence to the contrary. Instead of opening up our minds to the possibility of more, we tend to close our minds, stubbornly proclaiming that we have all the truth we need and that anything new—anything that shakes our current beliefs—must be squashed.

Is the World Flat or Round?

Not so long ago man believed that the world was flat. You can see why. Our physical senses say the horizon is flat, and most people only believe what their physical senses tell them. It was a huge leap for man to acknowledge that the world is not really what it appears to be.

We used to believe that our senses could detect all that was true reality. Now we know that there is a vast universe that lies outside our ability to perceive it because our senses are so incredibly limited. We can't detect sonar vibrations like dolphins. We don't see as well as eagles or even hear as well as our family pets. The truth is, there is a vast world that exists outside our physical senses. In fact, we wouldn't even know it was there if we didn't have microscopes and telescopes. Most of what we see, smell, taste, touch, and feel is only a fraction of what is actually present.

Developing Facts

Man once believed that the sun revolved around the earth. When Copernicus suggested that the earth was not the center of the universe, his life was threatened. Even 50 years later, when Galileo used a telescope to prove Copernicus's Theory, the church forced him to stand trial for heresy.

Man once believed that solid mass was really solid. Now we know that nothing is really solid and that everything in the universe is actually energy in motion. The chair you are sitting on is a dance of energy. The air you breathe, the food you eat, even the thoughts you think are alive with energy. Everything is energy!

New Possibilities

We used to believe that life just happens to us, but now through developments in quantum physics, we are discovering that the human mind is a critical part of the mix. Did you know that the mind actually influences and alters the properties of whatever it observes? That means we can no longer see ourselves as passive observers or victims of chance. We must now accept that this is a participatory universe. Moment by moment, we are literally creating our reality.

That's a long way to have come in just a few hundred years. But think about this. In every age, man always believed that he had evolved to the fullest possible understanding of the world in which he lived. The truth is that we are only at the beginning of understanding how things really work. The important fact is this: Your mind is so powerful that if you believe something is true, then it is true **for you**.

Do you want to hold onto old beliefs that one day, years from now, future generations will look back and shake their heads in disbelief at your lack of understanding? Or, do you want to open up your life to the possibilities that lie out in front of you? If you are willing to accept that we are living—like our forefathers did—with a limited understanding of how the universe really works, then you can free yourself from the programming of the past and allow amazing new frontiers to open up for you.

New Operating System

Our rational minds are founded in rational knowledge. It's what helps the mind discriminate, divide, compare, measure, organize, categorize, define, label, and evaluate. The mind needs that kind of structure. It wants to see the world in black and white, as linear and sequential. The problem is that the world does not fit into this kind of definable box. So how can our structured mind cope? It can't. It can't use rational thinking to understand a universe that is a formless, dynamic web of constantly changing energy that responds to the mind regardless of its ability to grasp the concept. So we must install a new operating system. We must upgrade our old programming to a new belief system. Just for fun, let's call this new system The Next Gen 1000.

The Next Gen 1000 will do the following:

- Allow for ambiguity and expansion because that is how the world works.
- Question the validity of limited thinking, no matter what the subject.
- Test out new thought patterns, knowing that is how you grow.
- Support you as you become a seeker—a mental explorer—going where no mind has gone before.
- Help you gain confidence in the power of your mind, to influence the world around you.

- Support you in changing, so you can ***Get Out of the Rut and on With Your Life.***

Focus and Attract

Okay, so let's get down to it. Here is how this works. You give your attention to something. That something could be a memory from the past, a current situation you are living right now, or even some mental image you are conjuring up about the future. Whatever your focus is on, that becomes your point of attraction. Why? Because you have opened the file and it is now active, alive, and vibrating like crazy. That vibration sends out signals and, like a magnet, it attracts anything and everything that is a match. In essence, you are getting more of what you are focusing on.

When you open a file on **fat**, you can't attract **thin**. They are not even close to the same energy. If you want to attract wealth, health, and happiness, you can't open files about lack, sickness, and sadness. It just doesn't work that way. Whatever you focus on, you get more of it. That's how things work.

Focused Fan Wins

I'll give you a great example. Nolan, one of my godsons, is a huge basketball fan. He loves the Phoenix Suns, but more specifically, he loves Steve Nash. Several years ago, before Steve won his first MVP award, the Suns were scheduled to come to Albuquerque, New Mexico, to play in a preseason NBA game. When Nolan heard that the Suns were going to be in town, he immediately started dreaming about meeting his hero and getting his autograph. It was so much fun to watch his enthusiasm and belief in his dream. We bought tickets, but the best seats we could get were in row 23. I knew that would not put him close enough for the face-to-face encounter he had in mind.

As the weeks went by, his confidence grew stronger. He got his mom to buy him a new leather basketball and a permanent marker for that moment when he would be close enough to ask Steve for his autograph. As the game day grew closer, I have to admit that I was a bit concerned about finding a way to **make** this happen for him. Nolan took his ball to school for show and tell, bragging to anyone who would listen that he was going to the game and that he was going to get Steve Nash to sign his ball.

The night of the game, we got to the stadium early enough to get him in position during the pre-game warm up activities. Nolan waited with hundreds of other hopefuls to get a moment of Steve's time. But it didn't happen. The team retreated into the locker room and we were ushered to our seats far away from the court. Now, I was really beginning to doubt the dream. We were 23 rows away with thousands of others who wanted the same thing we wanted. I could feel the moment slipping away.

I was about to prepare him for the eventuality that he might not get Steve's signature when I looked into his eyes. He was having a blast: laughing, smiling, and clutching that ball. He still knew it would happen, and I didn't have the heart to burst his bubble. Near the end of the first quarter, Steve came out of the game. We watched him walk to the end of the bench, put his warm-ups on, and lie down on the floor to stretch his back.

That's when I heard Nolan shout out, "Hey, there's Aunt Meredith!" He was pointing down toward the first row. Sitting close enough to almost touch Steve Nash was Nolan's aunt. I couldn't believe it. We called her on our cell phone and then sent Nolan down to sit with her. Of course you can guess what happened next. After a time out, when Steve was walking back to the huddle, Nolan stood up and said to him, "Hey Steve, can you sign my ball?" Just like that. He simply ASKED. I watched from half a stadium away in total shock as Steve Nash bent over him and scribbled his name on Nolan's ball.

Nolan taught me something that day. He wanted it, he dreamed about it, he expected it, he asked for it, and he got it. No struggle, no pain, no fighting, no pleading, no justifying. He didn't realize that what he wanted was highly unlikely to pull off. He just knew he wanted it and he fully expected to get it. Now every time I see that ball sitting in its glass container, I am reminded that expectation is a very powerful ally. I didn't have to make it happen for him, he just attracted it.

Don't take my word for it. Let's put the Power of Attraction to the test. Go to your notebook and find the tab called *This Stuff Works*. I want you to use this segment to record the matches in your life between your thoughts, beliefs, mental pictures and the real physical stuff that shows up in your life.

Activities

Find the Match

Remember when you were a kid and you played the game Concentration where you laid out cards and turned them over in pairs looking for a matching card? Well, this game is very similar.

Every morning you are going to think of two or three unique objects. Spend a few moments thinking about your objects in a lighthearted way. Just 15-20 seconds per object will do. As you move through your day, watch for signs of the Power of Attraction in action. When you see any of your items, say to yourself, "That's a match." You are working on becoming more aware of how the magnetic power of thought works, so you are looking for matches between what you think about and what you get. Soon you will begin to see these matches everywhere.

I had one just the other day. My friend and I were talking about using typewriters when we were in high school—how tough they were to use and what an amazing creation the desktop computer is today. That afternoon I was channel-surfing and came across a rerun of a VERY old game show. The contestants where playing for the grand prize of a brand new…you guessed it—TYPEWRITER. I smiled and said to myself, "That's a match. That is the Power of Attraction in action."

Remember, every day to pick three new things to focus on. Write them down in your notebook under the tab *This Stuff Works.* At first you can stick with objects; later, you can choose concepts, like love, abundance, joy, smiles, etc. Whatever you focus on, the Power of Attraction will bring you more of, so make sure it's something positive. By capturing these experiences in your notebook, you are building your confidence that what you focus upon, you attract into your life. The more evidence you get, the stronger this new belief will become.

You have got to ask.
Asking, in my opinion is the world's most
powerful and neglected
secret to success and happiness
Percy Ross

Chapter 4

Want It!

Did you know that desire is the engine that drives everything in the universe? Without desire, nothing would happen. Desire isn't the enemy that some have made it out to be. It's a natural result of being alive.

In each and every moment, every cell of your body is asking for exactly what it needs to thrive: water, food, exercise, and sleep. You know that feeling when you sense a yawn coming. There's no stopping it. Your lungs need more oxygen. When that urge overtakes you, no matter where you are, you have to yawn. That's exactly how all desire is born. The conditions of your life create an urge or desire, and immediately you instinctively begin moving toward fulfilling that desire.

Automatic Responses

Your lungs ask for air. They don't beg and plead or try to justify why they deserve oxygen again and again. They simply expand—which is their way of asking—and oxygen rushes in. Unless you pinch off your nose or hold a pillow over your mouth, oxygen will rush in every time, no exceptions. You don't have to think about it, worry about it, analyze it, justify it, or work hard for it; all you have to do is NOT resist it. That's how strong an ally desire is. It is the great asker. If you don't resist, all that you ask for can flow into your life just as effortlessly as oxygen flows into your lungs.

One of the first Bible verses I remember learning as a child was, "Ask and it shall be given, seek and ye shall find, knock and the door shall be opened unto you." That's a pretty bold promise, but over the years I have learned that it's absolutely true.

What You Want is What You Get

Let's take a moment and clarify what you want. One day while I was at my desk, I started to write down what I wanted. At first, I only wrote down the things I wanted but didn't have. Then I expanded my list to include those things that I already possessed to some degree, but simply wanted more.

The more I wrote, the more I asked for. The more I asked for, the more I wanted. The more I wanted, the more grateful I was for what I already had. The more grateful I was for what I had, the more I wanted. It was a vicious cycle. The more I focused on what I wanted, the more it showed up in my life. I remember riding an emotional high for weeks because I became conscious of what I wanted and watched all the ways those things appeared in my life. I was constantly looking for and, therefore, finding the matches.

Here is my list, including both tangible items and intangible qualities. Go through the list and highlight or underline everything with which you agree. Then add anything else you want that isn't on my list. Let's see if we can get your desire engine running.

I want more...

Love	Passion	Intimacy
Excitement	Energy	Creativity
Money	Wealth	Travel
Freedom	Friends	Achievement
Peace	Joy	Happiness
Laughter	Fun	Adventure
Health	Vitality	Enthusiasm
Security	Wisdom	Understanding
Confidence	Courage	Patience

As you look at the list, you might feel overwhelmed because there is so much that you want and you aren't sure how to get. The good news is that you don't have to work hard. You don't have to chase your desires and wrestle them to the ground in order to possess them.

How to Get More

I am going to show you how to attract and allow all the desires of your heart into your life. If you aren't living the life you desire, it is only because no one taught you how to work in cooperation with life and the natural laws of the universe to attract to yourself all that you want. It is really that simple.

Ask and it will be given. You have been asking. The big question is what have you been focused on? Don't get me wrong, there still may be *work* required, but it is not the kind of work to which you have become accustomed. This work is more mental and emotional than physical.

- Your work now is to learn the way things work and to reprogram your mental computer so you are in alignment with the natural flow of life.
- Your job is to challenge the old files, your old beliefs, and your old patterns that have brought you to where you are today, but won't take you to the next step.
- Your assignment is to appreciate what you already have, while you fire up your desire for more.
- Your challenge is to find ways to play and laugh more, so you place yourself in a state of allowing all you have asked for to flood into your life.

> *All that we are is a result of what we have thought.*
> Dhammapada

Now I know that sounds like the kind of work you can get into.

Since life itself causes you to ask, why bother to set goals or spend endless hours visualizing your wildest dreams? That's a great question. Goal setting is not what makes things happen; the creation process begins with the birth of your desire. Dreams help you pave the way to aligning your beliefs with your desire.

In other words, when we spend time daydreaming about our desires, we are actually creating a mental and emotional link between where we are and where we want to go. We are literally creating an energy pathway between what we want and what we currently have.

That is great news. That makes the job of creation very simple. Not always effortless, but very simple. It's simple in that our only job is getting into mental and emotional alignment with our desires. How much simpler could it be? Just focus on what you want.

Let's set a fire to your desires by giving them time to surface. Here are a few activities that will help you get started.

Recalling Childhood Dreams

Part 1 — Do you remember sitting around with your friends, when you were little, dreaming about what you wanted to be when you grew up?

I do. My friends and I played a game where we would try to outdo each other with bigger dreams and wilder ideas. I can remember lying awake at night trying to come up with something more outrageous than anything I'd ever dreamed before. I could be an astronaut, or a trapeze artist, or a fireman, or a professional basketball coach. Each day it was a new dream. I kept reaching further and further. I never once thought to myself, "Oh, Debbie, that's not realistic. How are you going to get the money for that?" Or, "Don't be silly, Debbie; you aren't smart enough to learn that." Or even, "Now, Debbie, you're a girl and girls can't do that." When I was little, before I learned to doubt myself, I just dreamed big dreams. I wanted to experience it all. I was a fearless dreamer.

Now, it's your turn. I want you to go back to a time when you had big dreams, when you wanted it all and were a fearless asker. If you can't remember a time when you were like that, then you are going to have to imagine it. Take a few minutes and list *EVERYTHING* that you ever wanted to be.

Imagine that you can have, or do, or be anything you want—no strings attached. If you could have it all, what would it look like? Don't censor your answers. Don't ask how. Don't let old doubt files influence what you write. Don't worry about what others are going to think. Relax and let your mind run wild and your heart sing.

Part 2 — Examine your list and see if there are any patterns in your early dreams. Look for a lifestyle or emotional qualities that each of these dreams would offer you. Here is an example of my personal dreams and the lifestyle or emotional qualities that they would provide for me.

- **Astronaut** — adventure, living life on the leading edge, being an explorer
- **Trapeze artist** — entertainer, risk taker, flyer
- **NBA Coach** — competitor, educator, and motivator
- **Fireman** — rescue worker

When I look at my list, I can see that all of the qualities of life that I desired, I now have. It's true—I never became an NBA coach or a circus performer, but I am a motivator and risk-taker. The qualities that I wanted as a kid make me feel alive and fulfilled. Today, I know I'm living my purpose because I'm living the **qualities** of my dreams.

If you are living a life devoid of the emotional qualities that pulled you as a child, you may need to find a way to bring them back into your life. These emotional drivers are what give your life a sense of purpose and fulfillment. The drive is not for the end result of being a doctor; it is in the quality of life that you imagined being a doctor would give you. Perhaps what you seek is to feel the thrill of helping others. You don't have to be a doctor to feel that quality. Don't get me wrong. If your dream is to be a doctor, then go for it! Don't ever settle for less than you want in life.

Discovering Your Deepest Desires

Now let's do some brainstorming. Let your mind run wild and reach for the stars. I want you to use a separate sheet of paper for each one of these lists. At the top of the first page, write **TO DO**. On the second page, write **TO BE**. On the third page, write **TO HAVE**, and on the fourth page, write **TO GIVE**.

TO DO

If you could do anything, what would you want to do?

Let your mind go crazy. What have you always dreamed of doing? Would you want to write a book? Swim with dolphins? Meet your favorite movie star? Take a bike tour across Europe? Join a ceramics class? Open your own restaurant? Learn a second language?

If there were no limits as to what you could do, what would you do with your life? What places would you visit? What experiences would you have? What new skills would you acquire? Write them all down. Write as fast as you can. If your mind stalls, ask yourself, "What else?"

If you can dream it, you can do it.
Walt Disney

TO BE
If you could become anybody, who would you be?

Would you become a great inventor or maybe a renowned artist? Perhaps, your secret passion has always been to become a rock star. Maybe, you want to be a stay-at-home mom or an entrepreneur.

Whatever it is, write it down. Don't worry. Your unique genius is only uncovered, if you are doing what you love. What would make your heart sing? If you could be anything, what would you become? Don't stop keep writing and reaching for more.

TO HAVE
If you could have anything, what would you want?

Would you want to build your dream home? Have you been eyeing a new car? Perhaps, you want a new laptop computer or digital camera. Maybe you want something less material—like a new partner or a new job. If I told you that you could have everything your heart desires, if you just write it down, what would go on your list? Don't hold back. Include big things like world peace and millions of dollars in your bank account; include small things like a new handbag. Write it all down.

TO GIVE
If you could contribute anything to the world, what would it be?

What would be your legacy? Do you remember when you were young, idealistic, and just knew you would help to change the world? What would you do? Would you discover a cure for cancer? Maybe you would develop a new miracle food to eliminate world hunger. Maybe your vision is closer to home, like sending your kids to an Ivy League school. Perhaps, you want to help your local PTA build a new playground. Do you want to write poetry that will inspire generations to come? Write it all down. Imagine that you have been blessed with everything on your "To Have" list. What would you share with others?

Liberating Your Dreams

Now let's look back at what you wrote and evaluate what I call the limited-thinking factor. Are there things that you thought of writing down but didn't, because your limited-thinking mind talked you out of it? Did you sensor yourself?

Let's take the lottery test and see. The purpose of this activity is to help you continue to develop bigger dreams, to expand your ability to mentally go for it. I want you to reach further than you have ever reached. We use the lottery because it releases your mind from having to defend or argue the limits of your current life circumstances.

Go back to each of the four lists and draw a line under the last item in each category, so you know where the limited thinking ends and true limitless possibilities begin.

Now close your eyes and imagine that you just won the lottery. You will be receiving a yearly check for 50 million dollars, starting TODAY. Now, let's try the game again.

TO DO

With a bulging bank account, what will you do?

With 50 million dollars in your bank account, there are now no limits—anything is possible. What do you want to experience? Where would you like to travel? What kind of experiences would you want for you and your loved ones?

TO BE

With unlimited funds, what would you like to become?

Would you like to go back to school, or start a new business? What new skills or hobbies would you like to learn?

Remember, you are NOW a multi-millionaire and anything is possible. What kinds of self-improvements would you invest in?

TO HAVE

As a millionaire, what do you want to possess?

If you said that you would build your dream house, notice if it is a different house now than the first time you wrote it down. Maybe the first time it was just a step up from where you currently live. But now that you know you have millions, what kind of a house would you build? Does the dream get bigger? That is the goal. When you see more possibilities, you tend to dream bigger dreams. So dream big. Get specific. How many rooms? Would you put in a library, a pool, and Jacuzzi? What about an exercise room? How would the kitchen be equipped? Be specific with your dreaming. Each new idea opens up more possibilities.

TO GIVE

How will you share your wealth with others?

We have come to my favorite part. You have everything you want. You are becoming the person you have dreamed of becoming. You are doing things you never before thought possible.

Now, let's talk about what you want to contribute. Do you want to give money to your favorite charity? How much would you give? Think BIG. You have millions, more than you could ever spend, so how would you share yourself and your gifts with the world?

Look at your answers. Did you dream bigger the second time? Good. Now you're getting the idea. In order to dream bigger dreams, you must eliminate the judging mind that wants to analyze everything and explain to you why you can't have your heart's desire.

Desires are a natural expression of life. Life expands because of your desire for more, so dream big dreams. Step one in creating the life you desire is to ask for it. Remember: Ask and it shall be given!

Chapter 5

See It!

Now that you know what you want, the next step is to create a mental picture of exactly what it looks like. I call this your VISION. Your vision is not the same as a goal or a strategic plan. A vision is something so clear, so filled with sensory-rich information, that you can feel it. A goal is usually a number or statistic, something that can be measured and evaluated. You can see your goal on the scoreboard of life and say, "Yep, I made it!" or "Nope, I missed the mark." The problem is a scoreboard can get you into a lot of trouble, because it rarely tells the whole story.

Scoreboard Statistics

My high school basketball coach taught me this important lesson one night when we were playing against our arch rival. Our goal was to win, of course; but as the game neared the end, it was obvious that we would not succeed. With four seconds left, our coach called a time-out and pulled us into a huddle. We were ten points behind and four seconds was clearly not enough time to make up the difference. Looking into our disappointed faces she said, "Girls, sometimes you have to redefine your vision. We wanted to win. We gave it everything we had, but we aren't going to make that happen today. We have a choice to make. We can just let the clock run out, or we can change our goal and go for it. We can still leave here winners. Let's run play number three to perfection and leave here with our heads held high."

In play number three, the point guard would have to catch the ball and shoot—all in one motion, without even a second to see the rim. It was a play that normally required six seconds; but, if we got a good pick, it was possible to pull it off in four.

The team stood in a circle and each player mentally envisioned her part, picturing our moves flowing perfectly together. When we finished, we looked up at our coach. She said, "Go out there and play like the winners you are."

I stood out of bounds, and with a slap of the ball, the team flew into motion. The inbound pass was perfect. I streaked across the court, brushing past my pick, and looked up just in time to see the ball flying back to me. Jumping into the air, I turned to face the rim and shoot in one fluid motion. The ball was still in the air when the buzzer went off. We stood like statues holding our breath, waiting to see what would happen. As the ball swished through the net, our team went crazy. We ran screaming to the bench where we piled on top of our coach. It was one of the most amazing moments of my young life.

As we celebrated our "win," the other team stood in stunned silence. They looked at the scoreboard and then back at us. They couldn't understand how we could be celebrating when the scoreboard clearly identified us as the losers. What they didn't understand was that the scoreboard didn't tell the whole story.

It's Never about the Numbers

Some people will tell you that it's all about the numbers. I believe that numbers, dates, and statistics are very limited measures of success. They represent scores that don't always measure the right thing. Perhaps the greatest weakness of numbers is that by themselves, they don't really inspire much passion or greatness.

Let me demonstrate what I mean. "Twelve!"

Did that inspire you? Well, of course not. Twelve by itself is not really that exciting, but what if I say, "In the next twelve pages, I will give you twelve secrets to attract twelve million dollars into your life within the next twelve months." Now I have your attention. That's because now you have a picture and that picture means something. Now your emotions are involved.

Power of Vision

A powerful vision creates a personal identity, determines your direction, unleashes your personal power and, when necessary, inspires others. One of the greatest visionaries of modern times, in my opinion, was Dr. Martin Luther King Jr. He had a dream and when he shared his dream of equality and freedom, people of all races were moved to action. Although I was only a little girl at the time, I remember watching him on television. I was so stirred by his speech that I wanted to march with him. I could feel the energy and passion his words created, and I wanted to be a part of it.

That is the power of vision. Victor Hugo, the famous French writer said, "Nothing is more powerful than an idea whose time has come." That's what a vision is; it is an idea whose time has come.

How many people do you think would have been inspired to get on trains and busses and travel across the country to march with Dr. King, if he had said, "I have a strategic plan"?

All he had was a dream. He had no idea how it would unfold. He didn't unveil a strategic plan with timelines and action items. He never once said, "This is how it will come about." Instead, Dr. King spoke will eloquence and grace, with persuasiveness and emotion about his dream. His words inspired pictures that still move us today. Now that's a visionary.

Walking on Fire

The first time I understood the power of a vision, to move me into action, was at a personal empowerment seminar I attended with Tony Robbins. The last night of the workshop Tony had scheduled an activity that would seriously challenge my beliefs about what was possible for my life. That activity was a fire walk. I couldn't get my mind wrapped around the possibility that it was even humanly possible to walk on red-hot coals without getting burned. When I opened my file on fire, it said, "Fire burns and that is a FACT." I could not see how it was possible to get around that fact.

No matter how eloquent his arguments were, my mind couldn't get past the HOW. How is this possible? Is it a trick? An illusion? Maybe the fires aren't that hot. My mind raced through a million possibilities, yet I found no comfort. Even as we moved outside to the 40-foot lines of red-hot coals and I watched person after person walk on the fire, I still couldn't understand how it was possible for me to accomplish it without getting burned.

As I looked around me, I saw others who must have been asking the same questions, because I could see the fear on their faces and the doubt in their eyes. That question, "How?" almost stole my opportunity for real growth that night, but something inspired me to change my focus. I got a sudden impulse to stop looking at the fear surrounding me, to ignore the heat of the fire, to stop asking how, and to look instead into the eyes of those across from me who had already walked the fire.

That's when I saw it. I saw belief in their eyes instead of doubt. I saw confidence instead of fear. I saw invincibility instead of vulnerability. I saw what I wanted most for my life—a knowing, a deep certainty that anything is possible. I knew that, if I walked, I would feel everything I wanted for my life was within my reach. I knew that if I lived my life with that kind of confidence, my wildest dreams really could come true. When I saw what I wanted and focused on why I wanted it, the next step was easy.

Gone was my fear. With an amazing sense of calm, I walked barefoot on glowing coals that were over 1,400 degrees—hot enough to melt aluminum—and yet I felt nothing. I was aware of nothing but the eyes of those at the end of the line calling to me. "Come on, Deb, you can do it!" I suddenly believed them; I could do it. I could have it. I could have anything I wanted. Nothing could stop me, not even the fire. Not something others would say was impossible.

I learned that night that, when I keep my eyes on the prize, fear and doubt disappear. That picture of what my life could be like, if I lived it from a place of possibility, was so powerful that the vision took on a magnetic energy and literally pulled me across the fire.

It didn't take discipline or hard work that night. I just had to align my mind and body with what I wanted, and almost magically, I felt the pull of inspiration to walk. There was a sense of perfect timing as a voice in my head said, "Now!" and I stepped out onto the fire, walking painlessly toward my vision, toward my desires. No fighting, no struggling, no pain—just a short 10-foot walk. That's the beauty and power of a vision. When you get into alignment with your deepest desires, you can simply answer the call of inspiration. Yes, action was required. I did have to walk, but I didn't have to force it. When you stay focused on your dreams, they literally call to you. Like a little voice inside your head that says, "Come this way." As long as you stay focused on your desires, they will call you across the fires of life.

False Files

I also learned that night that some of the files that masquerade as fact are actually nothing but phonies. My file said that fire burns, therefore, walking on fire without injury was impossible. I learned that what one person believes is impossible can be completely possible for another. That means that impossible is not a fact, but simply someone's opinion. That opinion comes from the limited thinking that goes on in a limited mind. I decided that night that I was never going to let the limited opinions of others control my mind again.

I also realized that my phony files felt very real. It was tough to distinguish them as phonies, because I had spent my whole life believing they were facts. I discovered that when I questioned one file it led me to question another and another and another. I had to ask myself, "If that file was a phony, how many other fact files were counterfeit as well?" How many other limiting beliefs had I believed? How many times had someone said to me, "You can't do that," and I downloaded that bogus belief, labeling it as fact? One by one the dominoes fell that night, as I questioned the validity of all of my old files.

Helpful Virus

What I discovered was that when you question a file, you infect it with a very powerful virus. That virus is called doubt. If you have strong empowering beliefs, obviously you want to keep doubt as far away as possible, but if you have a belief that limits your potential, doubt can become your greatest ally. So if you open a money file that says, "I will never get out of this hole," you can infect it with a doubt virus that says, "I don't know how, but I think it is possible to find a way out." That simple little thought is enough to give you some breathing room. It gives you a bit of hope. It opens you up to the possibility that help is on the way, and that's all you need to move forward.

I also learned that focusing on the question of "How?" limits my mental resources and separates me from my desire. Aligning with my desire was the most powerful thing I have ever done. I got to see firsthand the power of answering the question "Why?" The answer to that question connects you to your emotions.

Let me show you what I mean. Maybe you would say, "I want that new car because it will give me more freedom. I want that new job because it will increase my financial flow. I want a relationship because it will give me someone with whom to share the adventures of my life." The statement that comes after because is what adds punch and power to your desires and creates the emotional attachment.

Powerful Visions

Now that you know the power of a dream, it's time to help you create some powerful visions of your own. Remember, a vision is a vivid picture of the future. It's so vivid that you can close your eyes and see it happening. A vision statement transports you into a mental movie experience of what it will be like when your dream is fulfilled. A vision envelops your senses. You can see it, feel it, taste it, touch it, and smell it. You are there!

Below are some powerful statements from three great visionaries. See if you can catch a glimpse of the powerful picture in each dream.

Dr. Martin Luther King

> *I have a dream that one day on the red hills of Georgia, the sons of former slaves and the sons of former slave owners will be able to sit down together at the table of brotherhood...*
>
> *I have a dream that my four little children will one day live in a nation where they will not be judged by the color of their skin but by the content of their character...*
>
> *I have a dream that one day the state of Alabama... will be transformed into a situation where little black boys and girls will be able to join hands with little white boys and girls and walk together as sisters and brothers. ...*
>
> *I have a dream that we will be able to speed up the day when all of God's children, black men and white men, Jews and Gentiles, Protestants and Catholics, will be able to join hands and sing... free at last, free at last, thank God Almighty, we are free at last"*

That speech always gives me the chills. Did you see his vision? Can you feel his dream? He didn't talk in vague statements or use target dates and measurable statistics; he created a crystal clear picture of what that day would look like. You can see it, can't you?

President John F. Kennedy

Let's use another great visionary and look at his dream that captured the attention, desire, and drive of our country. More than

40 years ago President John F. Kennedy presented a challenge to the American people. His vision was to send a man to the moon. His words may not be as eloquent as Dr. King's, but his dream was equally as bold. His vision created a new identity and unified a nation. Here is what he said…

> *This is not merely a race…We go into space because whatever mankind must undertake, free men must fully share. I believe that this nation should commit itself to achieving the goal, before this decade is out, of landing a man on the moon and returning him safely to the Earth. No single space project in this period will be more impressive to mankind or more important for the long-range exploration of space; and none will be so difficult or expensive to accomplish.*

And with that the space race, which we were losing to the Soviet Union, got a huge boost. More than that, Americans had a new identity and purpose. We were going to do the impossible. We were going to be the first nation to send a man to walk on the surface of the moon, and we were going to do it by the end of the decade. That focus and united effort changed our country forever and on July 20, 1969, with five months to spare, we did it.

I remember sitting in front of our old black and white television set with the crooked rabbit ears, watching the fuzzy images from the moon. I was so inspired that I wanted to be an astronaut, too. That's what a powerful vision accomplishes. It creates a sense of identity, solidifies a common purpose, unifies the team, and when it is achieved, it moves us all to reach for more.

Roger Banister

A third example of a powerful vision is the story of a man named Roger Banister, a world-class runner in the 1950s. His race was the mile run. Roger decided that he was going to do the impossible. He was going to run the mile in under four minutes. Not only had this never been done before, but more than 50 reputable medical professionals told him that it was physically impossible. They advised against pursuing his dream, telling him that such a pursuit could cost him his life. They believed that the human heart could not withstand the stress that such a pace would require. Roger ignored their so-called expert advice and continued to believe that it was possible. He had his own vision of how it would happen, and he visualized his dream three times a day. In his book, he wrote...

> *The earth seems to move with me...a fresh rhythm*
> *enters my body. No longer conscious of my movement*
> *I discover a new unity with nature...a new source of*
> *power and beauty, a source I never knew existed.*
> *As I cross the finish line I see the timer and smile.*

After Roger accomplished the "impossible" and ran a mile in under four minutes, more than 45 other athletes accomplished the same feat during the next year and a half. Roger's vision inspired others to move past their limits and do what no one thought was possible.

Visions inspire others to reach for more and to believe in possibilities.

Creating Your Vision

Let's talk about the keys to establishing a powerful vision. First we will cover the keys to turning your deepest desires into inspiring visions, and then I will include an exercise for each of the following points to get you going.

#1. Your vision must be inspired by YOUR desire.

This has to be something you really want. If it's something someone else wants for you, or you want it because you think you should want it, or you think it would be nice but your heart is not really in it, forget it. It will never happen, and it will just reinforce the limiting thinking that you can't really achieve your heart's desire. You need to do some serious soul-searching to find something that you are truly passionate about. It should be something that pulls at your heart and calls to you in your dreams. These desires are the foundation of good visions. Without this deep desire, you will find it hard to stay the course when obstacles arise. Dr. King was passionate about his dream—so passionate that he never gave up, no matter what the cost. Lack of passion is the reason so many people abandon their dreams before they are realized.

Go back to the lists you wrote, in the last exercise, and cross out anything that is not YOUR desire. If it doesn't belong to you, it doesn't belong on your list.

#2. Your vision must be something BIG.

Dreaming big can be difficult because it causes our rational mind to kick in and try to analyze how our dream will be achieved. That is why you never ask the "How?" question during the dreaming phase. Dreaming big inspires greatness and calls forth big energy.

Dr. King envisioned equality and freedom in a time when people were dying because of the color of their skin. He had no idea how his vision would unfold, only that it would. President Kennedy wanted to put men on the moon when we hadn't yet even successfully sent a man into space. Most people thought his dream was lunacy. Roger Banister wanted to do something that doctors told him was beyond the realm of human ability. Thankfully, none of these visionaries let the current reality stop them from dreaming big and because they dared to dream, they inspired greatness in all of us.

Go back to your list again. Using a highlighter, identify all the items on your list that feel really big. These are the things that make your heart race when you think about them. If it causes your engine to race, your passion to fire, and your heart to sing, then you are on the right track. If there is nothing on the list that gives you those feelings, I suggest that you take a few of your desires and make them bigger.

#3. A vision serves as a beacon.

Dr. King focused on the end result, not the process of achieving it. That is because a vision shines a light; it calls to us. Notice that Dr. King said, "I see a day when…" Then he describes that day. He never tells the crowd what they should do, how they should behave, or what they should believe. He simply says, "I have a dream… and here is what it looks like." It is one of the most powerful speeches of our time, because it transported us to a moment somewhere, in the future, where we could actually experience what his dream would feel like.

You can temporarily consider what you don't want, but you must frame your vision in terms of what you do want. Avoid negative statements like, "I don't want the bill collectors calling me anymore." Instead, envision a day when you easily pay your bills on time and in full. Can you feel the difference? Once again, remember that now is not the time to worry about how; just focus on what you want and why you want it. There will be plenty of time to consider how, but for now, let's just find your dream.

Review the highlighted items and ask yourself are these the end result or the stepping stones along the way. Don't get me wrong. The stepping stones are a part of your desires and they are great, but right now we want to see what the end picture looks like. If you have only listed the stepping stones, see if you can envision where the steps are taking you. Can you describe the end picture?

#4. A vision is always positive and specific.

Dr. King didn't give a picture of what he didn't want; he didn't even say he wanted to wipe out racism. His words told what he wanted. He knew that he couldn't create a powerful magnetic vision and continue to talk about what he didn't want. He kept his eye on the prize.

While you are looking at your list, make sure that everything on it is what you want, not what you don't want. A vision of peace is different than a vision of stamping out violence.

When a client calls and wants to schedule me to come and speak to their organization, I always ask, "What do you want your people to walk away with?" I want a clear picture in my mind of how those people will feel as they leave my seminar.

I always create that end picture first. I close my eyes and see the event I want to create. I picture their smiling faces, I hear their laughter, and I feel their energy. I imagine participants coming up to me after my speech and saying things like, "That was the best seminar I have ever attended," or "I feel so good about myself right now," or "I feel like I can do anything." I always picture the end result and then from that picture, I plan my seminar.

Review: A Vision

1. Must be inspired by YOUR desire.
2. Must be BIG to call forth your greatness.
3. Must focus on the end result.
4. Must be positive and specific.

Activity 1

Picture Board

Start by reviewing your lists of desires from the previous chapter. Highlight the top ten on each list and use them for this activity. Creating picture boards is a great way to embellish your vision. If you are a visual learner, try collecting pictures that capture the visual images you are trying to create. I love to go to the bookstore and buy magazines that have pictures of things I want in my life. They can be small things like new electronic gadgets or big things like pictures of my dream home. I also like to cut out what I call *power phrases* that I find in magazines and newspapers. Taking the pictures and phrases, I paste them on colored paper to create a scrapbook image of what I want to attract. Having a picture board helps me hold the visual image of the end result in my mind.

Mind Movies

In the last chapter you did some brainstorming and you let your mind run wild to create a list of things you would like to do, be, have, and give. The next step is to turn them into a clear picture or vision. Go back and look at your lists of desires and pick something that has a strong pull. What would life look like, if you had already accomplished this dream? What would it be like to live your vision on a daily basis? See yourself inside the picture and describe it in as much detail as possible. When you script out your vision, you are literally acting as a scriptwriter for this mini-movie of your life. Write it so when you read it, it creates emotion within you.

Here is a great example of a script written by a woman who was working on a vision of experiencing the vacation of a lifetime. See if you can feel her vision.

> *I see my husband and me walking hand in hand on a beautiful Caribbean beach. The calm crystal clear water gently rolls in covering our feet. Turning to look at the burnt orange horizon, a gentle breeze blows in off the water sending thrill bumps through my body. I take a slow, deep breath, filling my lungs with the invigorating ocean air while I soak up this amazing moment.*
>
> *Tears trickle down my cheeks as an overwhelming sense of appreciation fills my body. Looking into my*

partner's eyes I see his glowing face and I know he feels it too. It is one of those moments that I have been dreaming of. It is a moment that I will cherish for a lifetime.

I am overcome with love and appreciation for this special moment. For I am standing on this island beach with the love of my life watching the most breathtaking sunset I have ever seen. I feel his strong arms surround me as we stand awe struck by the beauty that surrounds us.

That's an incredibly graphic script. Did you feel this woman's vision? Were you there with her? Notice she didn't talk about how she acquired the money to make the trip. She didn't even address how she attracted the love of her life, but you could feel that all of those things had happened. You were a spectator watching her movie unfold. More importantly, she was the lead actress living her dream.

Part 1 — Now it is time to script out your own movie. Pick one of the four categories or combine them in some special way and write a movie script for yourself. Spend a few moments every day embellishing the details of how it will feel. Use sensory rich language and be sure you capture every little nuance of the experience. What does it taste like? What sounds do you hear? What are the colors, texture, and shapes that you see? Make it 3D. Create your own widescreen HD experience. Make it clear, crisp, and real.

Read through and edit your script on a daily basis until it is perfect. The woman's script you just read was the result of her working daily for about two weeks. The more time you spend with it, the more real it becomes. The more real it becomes, THE MORE REAL IT BECOMES! Get it? Good.

Part 2 — Once you have pictures and your script, you can put them together to make a scrapbook of your vision. You can write scripts for several different areas of your life, or combine them into one storyline, but you want to create a model that you can tell your subconscious mind, "This is what I want my life to look like."

Once you have these mind-movie scripts written and illustrated, you need to read and look at them on a regular basis. In the beginning, it is a good idea to read over your vision scripts two or three times a day. Keep them by your bed, so you can review them in the morning before you get out of bed and at night before you retire for the evening. The more you visit your vision and put yourself into the picture seeing it as reality, the faster you will attract these components into your life.

Dream big dreams and get very clear about exactly what you want. Now is not the time to get bogged down in the details of how. Just spend time dreaming and defining your vision. Once that vision is clear, you will be delighted and amazed at how easily each "how" will become evident.

If we did all the things we are capable of doing,
we would literally astound ourselves.
Thomas Edison

Chapter 6

Think It!

Do you really want to know how powerful your mind is? Just look around you. The chair you are sitting on was once merely a thought in someone's mind. That car you drive was once just an idea. The money you use, all the things that money buys, even the emotions you feel are all the products of the mind. Everything that is in physical form now was once no more than a thought. All creation begins with thought, which means that every thought you think has creative power.

Matching Thoughts

If every thought has creative power, then the obvious next question should be, "What thoughts created my current life experience?" If your experiences are full of lack, fear, and hardship, I guarantee you have been thinking matching thoughts. Prosperous people don't indulge in deficit thinking. Happy people spend their lives thinking happy, optimistic thoughts; people who are miserable do just the opposite. It is really very simple—negative thoughts create negative results; positive thoughts create positive results. If you want to understand your life experiences, you must start by looking at your dominant thoughts. Changing your life begins with changing your dominant thought patterns.

My earliest exposure to understanding the power of thought came from my grandfather. I still remember his words of wisdom as though it were yesterday, "Debbie, don't ever listen to anyone who tells you that you can't. You can do anything you want to do, IF you think you can!" He was an enthusiastic fan of Napoleon Hill and his book, *Think and Grow Rich*. He was constantly filling his mind with empowering thoughts and inspirational material. I loved my grandfather so much— not so much for anything he ever did for me—but for how he made me feel about myself when I was with him. He knew that the single most important factor to having all I wanted in life was for me to understand the power of my thoughts.

Discovering the Power of the Mind

Napoleon Hill was one of the early pioneers of the current Power of Mind movement. He spent the best years of his life searching to understand why some men were successful and others were not. He interviewed the wealthy and powerful men of his time and found one common thread—they all understood the power of thought. They all knew that what they thought about would come about. They used their thoughts in a deliberate and conscious way to amass great fortunes and power.

The truth is that the power of thought is not really a recent discovery. All leading-edge thinkers throughout human history have understood that thoughts have creative power. Start at the beginning of time, read all the great philosophers, dive into all the ancient texts, review the lives of great thinkers, and you will find that this is truly old wisdom.

Mental Ruts

Thoughts have the power to create because they have the power to attract. Let's go back to the computer metaphor for a moment. When you have a life experience, your brain searches its hard drive for files to evaluate, explain, and categorize your experience. It finds a file and opens it. Now, remember, once you open a file or focus on a thought, that thought becomes active. This means it is sending out energy all over the place. That energy has "pulling power," so it literally attracts similar energy, thoughts, and experiences to you. Before you know it…BAM! You get what you are thinking about. If you are doing the daily "That's a Match" activity, I bet you have proven to yourself, by now, the power of your thinking.

Most of us think the same thoughts over and over again. That's because we get into habits or ruts, and our mind loves ruts. The truth is we learned very early, as part of our social programming, how to think. We mimicked the thinking patterns we were exposed to as children. Let me remind you that roughly 85% of the thoughts you think today are the same thoughts you thought yesterday. Well, that is quite a rut. We have patterns of thinking that are comfortable, and so we put our mind on auto pilot and just keep thinking the same thoughts we have been thinking for most of our lives. That's why we continue to get more of what we have always experienced.

Have you ever known someone who grew up with an abusive parent and then as an adult chose an abusive spouse? It's really not a big surprise. When we let our minds run on automatic, they run the same programs and think the same habitual thoughts, which of course, bring the same results. Those habitual patterns are the dominant thoughts that have pulling power to attract matching life experiences. That's the reason you must change your thinking, if you want to change your life.

This really isn't rocket science. It is deceptively simple. Thoughts fall into two basic categories.

1. Positive thoughts create positive results in your life.
2. Negative thoughts attract negative results.

I know it seems too simple to be true, but true wisdom is always simple. The tough part is becoming conscious of what we are thinking and then changing those mental ruts.

Bombarding Messages

Let me share another metaphor. Imagine that you show up on the planet and you are a free spirit. You think that anything is possible and that you are invincible—until you start having life experiences that make you question your greatness. Perhaps a neighborhood bully calls you a fatty, and as you stand in front of the mirror, you find a tiny little fold of skin around your belly which, in your mind, confirms his proclamation: You are FAT!

Maybe your teacher tells you that you are hopeless when it comes to math, and your failing math scores seem to prove this opinion of you.

Perhaps one night in the depths of her despair, your mom blames you for the fact that your dad walked out. Now in your broken heart and confused little mind, you decide that she must be right.

It doesn't stop there, as soon as you are old enough to process thought, you start picking up messages from advertisements that you are imperfect. Your life is full of authority figures that want you to think, believe, and behave the way they have decided is right for you. The truth is that you are bombarded on all sides with people telling you that you are not enough of one thing or too much of another. What your innocent, moldable young mind doesn't realize is that all of them have a vested interest in shaping your beliefs and, therefore, your behavior.

Destructive Declarations

Limiting statements are a constant in our lives. I know you have heard them. They might sound like this:

"You can't do that."

"You're not smart enough to accomplish that."

"You're just a girl."

"Boys don't cry!"

"You don't have the money or talent."

"Who do you think you are?"

It doesn't take long before your free spirit is bound by the limits others have assigned to you. Each limiting thought you accepted, as a child, became another bar of the cage that still imprisons you today. You need to understand that all oppression is self-created. Those bars are illusions. They are simply a shadow of dark, limited thinking. They cannot hold you in, unless...of course, you believe they can.

Your negative mind will always create thoughts with limits. That's what it does—what it has been trained to do. These negative interpretations are nothing but cultural programming.

Guess what? Programming can be changed. You can change the oppressive, limiting thoughts of your past. You can let go of the outdated ideas and negative attitudes that imprisoned you. You can use the most powerful asset you have, CHOICE! Yes, choice. You can choose to think something else.

Constructive Choices

You can choose to think positive thoughts. A positive mind sees possibilities and opportunities. A positive mind frees your spirit and allows your heart to sing. You can choose to be bold in your thinking. You can break free from the negative thoughts that have created negative results in your life. You can use the power of positive thought to create your heart's desires. Once a mind is free, there is no place it can't go and, since you create anything you think about, you can have anything you think about!

Notice what just happened inside your head. Did you roll your eyes and think to yourself, "Give me a break, Deb?"

Do you believe what I said, or are you blowing me off? The answer to that question is the key to your future. If you can believe that all you have to do is change your thinking habits, then you are well on your way to changing your life experiences. If you don't believe it, do me a favor and hang in with me for a bit longer. What do you have to lose? Test this out for yourself; don't let the limited programming of your past limit your future.

Let me be clear—you don't have two minds. You don't actually have a dark mind that creates dark thoughts (though sometimes it sure feels that way). The truth is that it's more like wearing a pair of dark, dirty, smudgy glasses. Looking through them alters the way the world looks. Rose-colored glasses will make you feel optimistic because the world looks bright and glowing; dirty glasses will make you feel oppressed because the world looks dark and stormy.

Illusion or Reality

Let me give you a better example. Have you ever seen a 3D movie? I took my godsons to Disneyland last summer and sat through the coolest 3D movie I had ever seen. The images jumped right out at me. Several times I literally screamed and ducked my head. I quickly took off my glasses and realized that what felt real to me was only an illusion. Those glasses tricked my senses into believing that what I was seeing was real. When I put the glasses back on, my brain sent signals to my body that said MOVE! Even though I knew it was an illusion; I still reacted.

You're having the exact experience every day. Your filters—which are your thought patterns, positive or negative—are telling you that your interpretations are fact. If you take off those dirty glasses, you will see that a whole other world exists. Your Limiting Thought Patterns (LTPs) can come from messages you picked up early in life. They might have been added to your programming, or they could be your own personal interpretations of life experiences.

Example: Sad Susie

I had a client; I'll call her Susie, who was always telling me that she didn't know what her dominant thoughts were. I told Susie that since her life was a reflection of her dominant thoughts, it would be easy for us to discover what those thoughts were. Her life was a perfect example of how the thoughts that she habitually practiced had attracted a life experience that matched her expectations. She had been abused as a kid and still has regular nightmares about being victimized, used, and abused.

I bet you can guess her life story. She has never had a serious relationship because she thinks all men are *out to get her*. She has been the victim of identity theft, her home has been robbed twice, and she was carjacked a few years back. She also had some of her professional writing plagiarized. Still, she couldn't see that her constant worry about being taken advantage of could possibly be creating her experiences. But you can see it, can't you?

Susie's LTPs caused her to live in constant fear. She completely rearranged her life to try to protect herself. Although she double-bolted all of her doors, paid for extra security for her home, and set her car alarm she still attracted thieves.

She would even do without something she sincerely wanted if she was required to give out personal information to get it. She limited herself to a cash-only world, terrified that someone could use her credit card information to find her. What she wanted more than anything was to travel to Europe, but she wasn't willing to file the paperwork for a passport. Talk about creating limits! Can you see how the thought, "People are always looking for ways to get me" kept her living in fear? It hasn't protected her; it has limited her. With a thought like that, she will never be safe. It doesn't matter how much security she invests in. Her fearful thoughts put her directly in harm's way every day.

Activity 1

Worry or Gratitude

Part 1. **Exploring Worry.** So let's see what NTPs (Negative Thought Patterns) are running through your head on a regular basis. Get your notebook out. I'll ask you a question, and you write down everything you can think of that causes you to worry. Do you worry about your children, your body, your job, your finances, your home, or your employer? Don't censor or evaluate your answers, just write. I'll get you started with some examples.

Worry is one of the most powerful Negative Thought Patterns available to your mind. If you indulge in worry, you can be guaranteed to get the very things you worry about. When you find a way to give up the habit of worry, you can begin to attract new circumstances. That's the power of attraction in action.

Worry is not the only NTP you can engage in. Others include fear, doubt, anger, resentment, revenge, judgment, impatience, distrust, jealousy, boredom, hopelessness, panic, dread, and even frustration. All of them qualify as thought patterns that will take you in the opposite direction of your desires. If you have life circumstances that you do not want, your first step is to look at what NTP could have contributed to it in the first place. A great question for this activity is to ask yourself, "Since I know that all my life experiences were created in my mind, what thoughts must have I been thinking to create this experience?" See if you can discover what thoughts you habitually think that have lead you to today's reality.

Part 2 — **Expressing Appreciation.** If worry is one of the most powerful NTP that you can engage in, what is the most powerful Positive Thought Pattern (PTP)? The answer is simple—appreciation. The intentional act of appreciating anything has the power to change your life in a significant and positive direction.

What do you appreciate about your home, your family, your children, your body, your job, or your employer? You may have to stretch a bit, but it's well worth the mental effort.

Let's talk for a moment about other PTPs. What thoughts would lead you closer to your dreams? Things like love, gratitude, certainty, excitement, calm, anticipation, happiness, expectation, confidence, peace, hope, bliss, pleasure, trust, desire, and joy.

I started this chapter with the statement that your life experience is the result of your dominant thoughts. So how can you tell where your current thoughts are leading you? That's an important question.

No pessimist ever discovered the secret of the stars,
or sailed to an uncharted land, or opened a
new heaven to the human spirit.
Helen Keller

Time Machine

Do you remember the old movie about the time machine? The creator of the machine would go forward and backwards through time. Let's play that game for a minute. Ask yourself this question, and then project yourself forward into the future and see if you like where it is taking you.

Pick any of your negative thoughts from the previous activity and imagine that you continue to think it for the next five years. Remember that what you think has creative power, so let's assume that you have attracted a life experience that is an exact match to your dominant thoughts.

Part 1 — **Identify a negative thought.** As an example let's use, "I'll never find the love of my life." If you continue to think this thought, how would you begin to feel? Hopeless? Unworthy? Resentful? Desperate? Not a pretty picture, is it? How attractive will you be to someone else if you feel needy and depressed?

Now you pick a negative thought of your own. Write it down and ask yourself, "If I continue to think this thought, how will I begin to feel?"

Next ask yourself, "If I continue to think and feel this way, where will I end up in five years?"

Is this what you want your life to look like? If the answer is no, then the solution is easy—you need to change your thoughts.

Part 2 — **Think positive thoughts.** Let's try the same activity with a positive thought. What would happen if you exchanged negative thoughts for positive ones? Exchange, "I'll never find the love of my life," with "My perfect mate is out there looking for me. The happier I become the faster he will arrive."

If you thought this thought every day, how would you begin to feel? Hopeful? Excited? Motivated? This kind of thought would put you into a state of anticipation. Do you think the outcome would be different?

So let's see if you can come up with a positive replacement thought for the negative one you listed above. Knowing the magnetic ability of thoughts, what would this positive thought attract to you?

Let a man radically alter his thoughts
and he will be astonished at the rapid transformation
it will effect in the material conditions of his life.
James Allen

Chapter 7

Feel It!

Have you ever heard the phrase *"living in the now"*? When I first heard it I thought it was a bit redundant. Where else would you be living? I have come to learn that the mind doesn't understand the difference between a memory, a current condition (one you are observing), or a future event (one you are imagining). That's right – the past, the present, and the future are truly all the same to the mind.

It sounds confusing, but it's really rather simple. Let's go back to our file-folder metaphor for a moment. Right now your brain has a file open; the question is, which file is it? As we have already seen, it depends completely on what you are focused on at this particular moment. For the sake of demonstration, I want you to recall a time when you felt powerful. Close your eyes and let your mind wander through your past and find a memory that makes you feel strong when you think about it.

Climbing the Rope

For me, one such memory would be when I was in gym class in first grade. My teacher, Mr. Fuller, was letting us climb the rope for the first time. He let the boys go as high as they could but kept stopping the girls when we got just a few feet off the ground. He kept telling us that no first grade girl had ever made it to the top. He said we were too weak and small and that we didn't have the courage or strength to be so high off the ground.

I was determined to be the first girl in the history of the school to touch the ceiling. When it was my turn, I climbed as fast as I could. The coach kept saying, "Okay, that's far enough." But I didn't listen and kept going. As I climbed beyond his reach, I could hear a bit of panic in his voice. "Girls can't climb that high. It's not safe." But his words meant nothing to me.

I had to stop a few times to readjust my grip. Each time I did, he told me to come back down. Refusing to quit, I kept climbing. When I reached the top and touched the ceiling, a feeling of electricity flooded through my body. I had done it! In that moment I knew that nothing was impossible for me. As I slid down the rope, Mr. Fuller's voice faded into the background. Even though he sent me to sit in the corner for not obeying him, I was floating on the clouds. I didn't care that I had rope burns on my legs or splinters in my hands. None of the minor pain or punishment mattered. I had proven to the world that a *girl* could climb to the top of the rope. I had proven to myself that I could do anything.

As I review my life, I realize this was actually the beginning. My dad often said, "Once Debbie puts her mind to something, you might as well get out of the way because she IS going to do it."

As I was writing my rope story, I felt goose bumps tingling all over my skin, the same way I felt as a victorious first grader so long ago. I felt the thrill of accomplishment again as though it had just happened. Closing my eyes, I can see defiant little Debbie with her fist in the air, determined to be the best. It doesn't matter that it happened 50 years ago. When I open the file and "relive" it right now, I am using my present moment to focus on my power, even though the event is in the past. My mind doesn't know the difference and, quite frankly, it doesn't care that it's only a memory. I gave it a command—find a feeling of empowerment—and it went out and retrieved a file. It feels as real to me now as if it were happening right now. That's because to the mind, it IS real.

Your Worst Nightmare

The same thing happens when you are daydreaming or imagining. Let's pretend that your 17-year-old daughter is late getting in from her date. You start to worry. You think to yourself, "Where could she be?" Your mind can't stand an unanswered question and so you begin speculating. You open a file labeled *My Worst Nightmare* and off your mind goes.

Does this dialogue sound familiar? *"Where could she be? She knows I worry about her when she is late. It's not like her to forget to call. Maybe she can't call. Maybe they ran out of gas. Maybe they are stranded on the side of the road somewhere. Maybe they have been in an accident. Maybe she is lying on the side of the road bleeding to death...."*

Your heart is pounding and the adrenaline is racing through your body as you picture her there in the heap of twisted metal taking her last breath. Then you hear a key in the door and you are snapped back to the reality of the moment. She is home and, for only a moment, you sigh with a feeling of great relief; then you jump to feeling angry with her, not simply for being late but for making you worry.

The truth is that nothing really happened, except that your mind got carried away with creating a fantasy so real, to you, that you actually experienced physical distress. That's because the mind doesn't care if what you are focused on is real or imagined. It can't distinguish the past or the future from the present. If you have opened the file and are thinking the thoughts, you will get the same feeling response.

Reviewing the Past

Let's talk about the past for a few moments. Like most of you, I experienced my share of childhood trauma, but after years of therapy I came to realize that nothing could change the facts of what I had experienced. I spent the better part of ten years working through my past. It all began in my early thirties when the depression I had lived with most of my adult life became debilitating. As my therapist and I explored the emotions beneath the depression, I uncovered a fear that felt truly life threatening. It gripped me with a stranglehold so tight I couldn't breathe.

Recognizing my fears moved me from depression and hopelessness into feelings of anger and revenge. I desperately wanted someone to pay for my pain. I put my parents through some tough years, as they became the easiest targets for my blame. Through the years, as the anger subsided, a deep sadness permeated my entire being. I cried at sad movies and happy movies. I cried if someone was rude or when someone was kind. I cried for no apparent reason at all. I cried and cried until I was sure there were no more tears, and then I cried some more.

After two decades of working through my memories, I have discovered that everyone has had painful experiences and that life is really about working through those memories moment by moment. The job is never really done because life triggers things in your files that you didn't even know were there. Your brain has woven a web of interconnected events and emotions. No matter how many years you spend in therapy, you will never unravel it all. The good news is that while it sometimes helps to understand where negative thoughts, opinions, and emotions come from, you will find that sooner or later understanding isn't enough. Just because I may have a really good reason for feeling fear, doesn't mean I want to or need to continue to let fear run my life any longer.

I have come to appreciate and make peace with the pain of my past. It is part of what has made me who I am today. I have made my share of mistakes - many I'm not proud of but all of them have made my life a rich tapestry from which I have grown into the woman I am today. I have found a way to use my past to create my present and eventually to serve my future.

> *What this power is I cannot say. All I know is that it exists...and it becomes available only when you are in that state of mind in which you know exactly that which you want...and are fully determined not to quit until you get it.*
>
> Alexander Graham Bell

Activity 1

Past Files

Part 1 — **Sights, Sounds, Smells.** Open your notebook. Take a few moments to let your mind wander back through the years. Look for the files listed below. Then take a few minutes to explain the experience in as much detail as you can remember. Describe each of your memories just like I did with my memory of climbing the rope. What were the specific sights, sounds, and smells?

Negative Files

1. Open a file that holds one of your most fearful moments.
2. Open a file that holds one of your most embarrassing moments.
3. Open the file on the worst day or moment of your life.

Positive Files

Now repeat the same exercise with positive files.

1. Open a file that contains an empowering moment.
2. Open a file that holds one of your happiest memories.
3. Open the file on the BEST day or moment of your life.

Part 2 — **Feelings.** Now go back to each of the memories and label the files with the emotions you felt then and the emotions you feel now when you remember the past. Later in this chapter, we are going to talk about the power of your emotions. But for now, I want you to identify those feelings.

Recognizing the Present

In order to make the most of this moment, you must be in the present: awake, aware, and alert. What I really mean is that you must pay attention. Most people allow their minds to run uncontrolled, allowing events going on around them to steal their focus and control their mood. If you don't make conscious choices about where to concentrate your attention, then whatever is creating the biggest commotion will capture your focus.

The truth is that your brain processes thousands of different stimuli every second. That's right; all of your senses are constantly feeding your brain information. Here is one of the most profound understandings I will share with you: your brain has a powerful filtering system that evaluates each piece of information that your senses pick up. Watch, I'll show you.

Look around the room for five seconds and count everything you see that is BLACK. Ready, go!

Good, now keep your focus on this page and without looking around the room again see if you can recall all the objects you saw that were BLUE. Not as easy as it sounds, is it? Look up and see all the blue items that surround you. Your eyes saw the blue, but your brain said, "Never mind! We are looking for black." It sifted the "blue" information out since it was not needed. The brain is a great tool. It helps you see exactly what you are looking for, but you need to understand how it works.

When you think a thought like, "I'm so ugly," your brain opens the file on *ugly*. Let's say that someone gives you a compliment. She says, "That blouse is such a great color on you. You look radiant in green." Your brain takes that information, sends it through the sorting system, and discards it as not a match to the dominant thought you think that says, "I'm so ugly." So when you receive this compliment, your brain literally blows it off. If a dozen people say you look stunning, and a single person jokes about you having a bad hair day, guess whom you believe. Once you have decided what to think, your brain will sift and sort through all the life experiences.

It will discard anything that is a contradiction to your beliefs, but will highlight everything that supports your dominant thoughts. It tries to bring you more evidence to prove what you already believe.

Turning Off Your Autopilot

If you don't pay attention to the signals in the present moment, it's a bit like putting your mind on autopilot. You are allowing the programming of your mind to control your destiny. Your mind gets in a rut and keeps thinking the same thoughts, which will bring you the same results over and over again. Is that really what you want? If you want something different, then you have to get your mind out of the rut, turn off the autopilot, and make conscious choices in each and every moment.

The present moment is a product of the past and a seed for the future. In every moment, you are planting a seed for a future experience.

So what are you planting?

- Are you thinking thoughts that bring you joy, or are you focused on things that make you feel sad?
- Are you remembering life experiences that make you feel powerful or reliving memories that make you feel like a victim?
- Are you counting your blessings today or worried about the unknowns of the future?
- Are you enjoying every breath you take, or counting the aches and pains that seem to mount every day?

Imagining the Future

If you are thinking about your future, you are daydreaming, visualizing, or imagining; all are powerful tools for creating your future. Don't forget, your mind does not know the difference between a memory, an observation, or a daydream—so, if you are going to fantasize, make sure that you are imagining success. When you fantasize failure—call it worry—you are actually creating what you are focused on. With that in mind, worry really doesn't make any sense. Worry will never help you solve a problem or avoid a catastrophe. All it does is pave the way for you to arrive at your "worries."

When you are imagining your future, you must always expect the best. The most powerful place you can be is in an attitude of excited expectation. If you can find a place of enthusiastic anticipation for your future, then you will be delighted when it arrives. Since life is always a self-fulfilling prophecy, the best question you can possibly ask yourself is, "Is the picture that I am holding in my mind what I want to experience?" If not, you need to make a u-turn and find a better thought or picture.

Activity 2

Describing and Labeling

Part 1 — **Obsessions.** Write a short description of each of these files. Describe in as much detail what you focus on when you open each of the files. What do you obsess over or worry about the most?

1. Strongest "worry" file.
2. Favorite "daydream" file.

Part 2 — **Emotions.** Label each of the above files with the emotions you feel as you think about them. See if you get any physical symptoms as well. Does your stomach hurt or your breathing quicken? Do you get a headache or do you break into a smile? Pay attention to the little signals your body is sending you when you focus on negative or positive files.

Feelings as Your Guide

Sometimes it's hard to know exactly what thoughts you are thinking. That's because our thoughts become habitual. Once you get into a mental rut, it's hard to even identify your dominant thoughts. That's where feelings come in. Believe it or not, your emotions are your truest guide to help you identify the thoughts you are thinking.

Here is how it works. First you clearly decide what it is that you want. Next you create a strong, positive, powerful picture of it in your head. What happens next is truly remarkable. You have a feeling and your emotions tell you if you are getting closer to or further away from your desire.

Geocaching with a GPS

I'm reminded of an experience I had last summer when I participated in a digital treasure-hunting game called Geocaching. It works like this. Someone hides a little treasure box somewhere in the world. Then they post the coordinates online and other people try to find it. There are hundred of thousands of little treasures hidden all over the world. I discovered that there were even geocaches in my neighborhood park.

It's not difficult to become a participant. You select the cache you want to find and program the coordinates into your GPS.

After programming the coordinates, the GPS guides you, step by step, directly to the treasure. It can do that because it knows where you are now, and it knows where you want to go. Those are the two most important pieces of information you need to find **your** treasure as well.

Amazing Machine

You have the same system hardwired directly into you, except your emotions are your guidance system. Once you have programmed into your mind what you want, the search begins. When you are on track, your guidance system sends you positive emotions to encourage you and keep you moving forward. When you are off track, you get negative indicators to tell you to turn around. When you feel joy, peace, love, or appreciation, you're on track. When you feel anger, frustration, sadness or revenge, consider it a sign that your guidance system is telling you to make a u-turn and get yourself back on track.

When I feel negative emotion, I imagine a huge STOP sign in front of me. Once I'm able to stop the negative mind chatter in my head, I picture myself sitting in my car at a four way stop. I can continue through the intersection on the negative path I'm currently on, or I can choose another direction.

When I look ahead I always imagine a dark, stormy sky and another sign that says DEAD END. I know that if I stay on this course, it will definitely not lead me to my dreams.

When I look to the right or to the left, I see clear blue skies. Now I get to choose which direction I want to take, knowing that when I turn away from the negative thinking I can follow my emotional guidance system to find my own treasure—every single time!

Let's investigate what emotions you feel on a regular basis.

Your GPS System

Part 1 — **Files and Feelings.**

1. Go through the two lists below and **circle** each word that you feel on a fairly regular basis when you open your file labeled *Money*. Add any words that are missing that should be there. Do that now.
2. Next, go through the list again and **underline** each word that you feel on a fairly regular basis when you open your file labeled *My Body/My Health*. Make sure you add any words that feel right.

3. Now go through the list again and put a **box** around each word that you feel on a fairly regular basis when you open your file labeled *My Relationships/My Love Life*. Feel free to add words that fit for you.
4. Go through the list one more time. Open any other file that is important to you. Now go through the lists and **highlight** the words that describe how you feel when you think about that file.

Negative/Limiting Emotions

Bored	Impatient
Worried	Vengeful
Insecure	Depressed
Judgmental	Pessimistic
Overwhelmed	Guilty
Defensive	Fearful
Grief-stricken	Jealous
Desperate	Sad
Frustrated	Hateful
Disappointed	Angry
Discouraged	Unworthy
Powerless	Limited
Hopeless	Doubtful
Helpless	

Positive/Liberating Emotions

Confident	Excited
Empowered	Creative
Optimistic	Inspired
Grateful	Lighthearted
Invigorated	Stimulated
Eager	Enthusiastic
Successful	Important
Content	Peaceful
Healthy	Joyful
Blissful	Happy
Loving	Lucky
Satisfied	Free
Hopeful	

Part 2 — **Desired Emotions.** Now go back and look at the words in both the positive and negative categories. Answer these questions for yourself.

- What emotions do I feel most often?
- What emotions do I rarely feel?
- What are my emotional default settings?

Look at the emotions that you don't feel on a regular basis, but would like to feel. Ask yourself, "What would I have to think in order to experience that feeling? What would I have to focus on in order to have that emotion be a part of my life on a regular basis?"

I'm asking you to look at the main emotions that you feel and discover what is missing. What would you like to feel more? Take out your journal and record your answers.

Some people say, "Well, if this condition would just change, I could feel better." I know you would, but unfortunately that's not how things work. You have to find a way to feel better first and then the results you want will show up in your life. When you are feeling good, you are on track and when you are feeling bad, you are off track. Like a metal detector that beeps louder when you are close to a hidden object, your emotional detector will give you all the good-feeling indicators as you move closer. It's as if your system is saying, "YES! Keep moving in this direction."

Check-up Time

Have you been writing daily in your *Joy Journal*? If you haven't, now is the time to start. Open your notebook to the *Joy Journal* tab and start writing all the things you have to be grateful for right now. Notice how it makes you feel. If you spend a few minutes a day looking for things you appreciate, you will start feeling more of those positive emotions. Watch how fast you can change your emotional state by looking for things that feel good!

If you want to be happy,
set a goal that commands your thoughts,
liberates your energy and inspires your hopes.
Andrew Carnegie

Chapter 8

Believe It!

A belief is nothing more than a habit of thought which your mind accepts as true or real. Beliefs are critical to your success, because you are what you **believe**. Yet, beliefs are not the unchangeable, solid facts they appear. If beliefs are merely habitual thought patterns, they should be easy to change, right? Well, not necessarily easy, yet incredibly simple. It's simple to change a habit since all you have to do is stop doing it, or do something else. That's about as simple as it gets, but simple is not always easy.

As we have already discovered, the mind holds on tightly to our beliefs. It will even sift out new information if it threatens those beliefs. Think of it as a security system that doesn't want its existing files to be compromised. That's why you must make a conscious choice to change. Your habits have gotten you into ruts. The only way out is to consciously choose something different. Here is the great news: once these new choices become habitual patterns, the same security system will shore the new thoughts, emotions, and beliefs. What once worked against you can now work for you.

Power of Belief

First let's talk about the power of your beliefs. We have learned that thoughts are creative. Did you know that habitual thoughts, which you absolutely 100% believe in, are even stronger creators? Let me give you a personal example.

From the time I was little, all I really cared about was playing sports. My mom, who was my first coach, used to say, "Debbie can pick up a racket, club, paddle, bat, or ball and play any sport better than most people who have been playing for years. She's a natural."

It was true, too. In high school I lettered in five sports. I felt like I belonged on the court, but put me in a classroom or social setting and I became extremely self-conscious. I fumbled, stumbled, and tripped my way through life feeling like I was a fish out of water. My belief was that I was a total klutz.

Now that you know how the power of attraction works, you can imagine how that belief shaped my life. I have countless stories of humiliating moments where I embarrassed myself in social settings. Each experience convinced me that my belief—**I am a klutz—** was FACT. Let me tell you one of my favorite stories, because it demonstrates the power of the mind to literally create exactly what we believe.

The Mind Matches Files

After graduating from Illinois State University with a degree in education, I moved to New Mexico to begin my teaching and coaching career in a small mining town. After a few glorious years, I lost my job as a PE teacher and coach because the mines began to close and the school district cut out all the "extras." I moved to the big city and started a new career in sales. To my surprise, I was a natural. All I had to do was knock on doors, have fun with people, and the deals just kept closing. After my first year as a salesperson, I was told that I would receive a special award at the company's annual awards banquet to be held in Chicago.

At first I was excited; it felt like high school all over again. I remember going to the athletic banquet during my freshman year and receiving my first major trophy—Athlete of the Year.

My heart quickly sank as my boss told me that the Chicago event was a formal, corporate affair. My old belief reared its ugly head. I just knew that going to such an event would be a major mistake. I started worrying. Every night before bed, I would imagine all the horrible things that were sure to happen.

Never having been to a formal awards banquet, I had no idea what to wear. So, I took my best friend shopping with me. This was back in the late '70s when women were wearing pumps with skinny 6" heels and polyester suits. After a nerve wracking shopping experience, I arrived at the banquet in a skirt that was so tight I could hardly separate my thighs. The combination of the toothpick heels and the skin-tight skirt caused me walk like a penguin. I couldn't have been more miserable.

As the evening progressed, I became more and more agitated. Seated at a table in the back of the huge banquet room, I knew I had to make my way through the maze of tables to get to the stage, but the worst was yet to come. When the emcee got ready to announce the awards, the house lights were dimmed. Two strobe lights, mounted on each side of the stage, began searching the audience until they settled on the winner and followed him or her to the stage.

Not only would I have to walk to the stage; I would have to do it in the dark with strobe lights in my eyes. I could feel panic beginning to grip me. My breathing became fast and shallow; my hands started to sweat and shake; my eyes felt as though they would pop right out of my head. Then it happened—the emcee announced in a booming voice, "Rookie of the Year – from Albuquerque, New Mexico – Deb Erickson!"

I froze in my seat; I knew something horrible was about to happen. I leaned over to my date and said, "Watch me do something stupid like trip on the stage."

I made it safely through the maze of tables and approached the stage. Gingerly I climbed up the first three steps, but on the last step my skinny little heel got caught in a crack. I stood paralyzed for a moment and then instinctively began to fight with my shoe. I yanked with all my might and the shoe gave in. The heel popped off. My shoe slipped off my foot and flew across the stage almost hitting the emcee in the head. That's not the worst part of the story.

When I tried to force my shoe loose, I lunged forward and did a beautiful chest-first dive across the stage. I slid so far and fast that my momentum caused me to slide right into the feet of the emcee at the center of the stage. He proved to be quite a character. I'm sure he was desperate to break the tension so he pretended to be a baseball umpire, threw his arms out and yelled, "SAFE!" That's not the worst part of the story.

Do you remember the old polyester? The material was very loosely woven, and the threads had a bad habit of catching and snagging. When I hit the stage, my suit grabbed the floor, but I kept right on sliding. As I slid, I heard the worst sound I could possibly imagine. My skirt split, from the back slit just below my knees, all the way up the seam to my waistband. I sprang to my feet. Holding my skirt together in the back and with one shoe on, I hobbled over to the podium.

I tried to compose myself and act as though nothing had happened, but when I looked up at the crowd to deliver my acceptance speech, I was devastated. They were laughing so hard that women had mascara trails running down their cheeks, men were falling off their chairs, and several women were running out the door. I can only imagine that they were escaping to the bathroom.

Years later a friend asked me what happened. Of course, I tried to think of someone or something to blame. I said, "It was that heel." But it wasn't the heel. It was my head. I had said, "Watch me trip," and my brain went in search of a matching file. I believed that I was a klutz and my mind made sure that my beliefs became my reality.

Power of Attraction at Work

Here are the facts. Your brain and body work together as a powerful team. Your brain says, "See this? Go get it," and your body delivers. Your brain actually sends chemical messages to your muscles to match the picture in your mind. But it doesn't stop there. The power of attraction will bring you all kinds of matches to whatever you are "ordering" with your thoughts.

If you say, "I can do this," your brain says, "Okay," and sends you everything you need to succeed. Confidence, coordination, power, agility, clarity, and enthusiasm—all of these qualities rush toward you from every corner of the universe.

If you say, "I can't do this," your brain says, "Okay," and sends you everything you need to fail—doubt, fear, confusion, weakness and, in my case, klutziness. Flip Wilson was right when he said, "What you see is what you get." The pictures or beliefs you hold in your mind are like little messengers sending out your requests.

Of course I didn't understand it back then, but now I know I was headed for trouble the moment I started worrying about attending the event. I now know that I could have turned it around in an instant, if I had listened to the warning signs my emotions kept sending me. The stomachaches, the sleepless nights, the near panic attacks should all have gotten my attention. My emotional guidance system was screaming at me, "Hello! You are headed down a dead-end street! This is not the direction you said you wanted to go."

Let's talk about your beliefs. Many different terms have been used to describe them. Some people talk about your core beliefs, global beliefs, and even foundational beliefs. Don't get caught up in the titles because some words are loaded and tend to set you up to struggle with this more than you need to. Beliefs are thoughts that you have practiced over and over, and so they feel real. They are NOT permanent. The only reason they feel solid and permanent is because you keep thinking them. You can change them right here, right now, if you want to.

Discovering Your Core Beliefs

Core beliefs are those that the mind accepts as absolute fact. This unquestioned programming becomes the foundation upon which all other beliefs and life interpretations are built. Imagine a great pyramid with each of these categories building upon the next.

The base or foundation is the largest and the tip the smallest. Let's call the base of the pyramid *The Game* and the top *My Future.* I'll give a brief description of each of the categories, and then you go to your notebook and write down your beliefs in that category.

The Game — This is the purpose of life and the nature of reality. This includes your belief in a Supreme Being, God, Source, Higher Power, or the lack thereof. It defines your relationship with the Creator and God's relationship to you. This is a critical category since it really defines you in relationship to all that is. Take a few moments and list your core beliefs about you and Source.

Examples:

- I am one with all that is.
- I command creative energy in my life.
- Jesus is my Lord and Savior.
- I am a child of God.
- I am alone in the Universe.

The Rules — This category is built entirely upon the first category: The Game. It explains how things work, identifies the rules of the game, explains consequences, and establishes rewards. In a nutshell, it gives you the scorecard upon which you evaluate your life. Look at the examples listed below. Then go to your notebook and ask yourself, "What rules govern my life?"

Examples:

- All rewards are in Heaven.
- God's laws rule my life.
- Life is short; you must leave a legacy.
- Life is eternal.
- I define what is right and wrong for my life.
- No pain, no gain.

- What goes around comes around.
- There is no free lunch.

The Players — This category builds on the previous two by further defining how you specifically fit into the picture. It defines who you are and who others are in relationship to you. What are the labels, limits, and boundaries of life? What roles, values, and potential do you and others bring to the game? This identifies what you can expect from life. Look at the examples below and see if any of them are true for you. Once again, use your notebook to add all the "I am…" and "People are…" statements that come to mind.

Examples:

- I'm a loser, a victim of chance.
- I'm only a woman. I don't really expect much.
- Bad stuff just happens to me.
- People are always looking out for number one.
- I can do anything I put my mind to.
- Anything is possible for me.
- I am responsible for all my life experiences.

My Past — This category covers your beliefs and interpretations of the events of your past. Many people are imprisoned by their past. Two people can have the same life experience and define it differently. One can see it as devastating and the other can label it as life changing. How do past experiences shape your beliefs today?

Here are a few ideas; now you write your own.

- I'm a lousy speller.
- I'm a total klutz.
- I'm weak and vulnerable.
- I'm a survivor.
- I'm unbeatable.
- I always land on my feet.

My Now — This category is your current point of power and, therefore, is the most important. What you believe right now is all that matters. It doesn't matter what you believed last year or yesterday or even a moment ago. What do you believe right now? I often work with people who tell me that they don't have positive beliefs at the moment, so we work on the beliefs they wish they had. Sometimes it helps to think about what you want to believe, so let's look at what you want for a moment. What can you add to this list?

- I want to believe that my life has purpose and meaning.
- I want to believe that I can change.
- I want to believe that my body can continue to heal and become stronger.
- I want to believe that my abundance is on the way.
- I want to believe that the past does not have to control my future.
- I want to believe that I can have it all.

My Future — This category, the top of the pyramid, considers what you believe is possible for your life. Life unfolds according to your beliefs, so what you expect is virtually what you will get. If you lived your life in a perpetual state of positive expectation, what would your future look like? Take a few moments to consider what beliefs about your future would inspire you to find your greatness?

- I am an amazing woman whose talents and gifts can change the world.
- I am a powerful man whose tender heart can inspire every life I touch.
- My future is so bright that I should wear shades.
- Anything is possible.

Activity 2

Matching Your Beliefs

Now go back through your beliefs and ask yourself these questions, "Where will this belief lead me? Does this belief empower me or limit me?" Let's work on one example together.

People are only looking out for number one. If you truly believe that everyone is looking out for herself or himself, what kind of people will you keep attracting into your life? Exactly—people you can't trust. As you continue to rub shoulders with selfish, shady characters, you could become a cynical, suspicious person who is always looking over your shoulder. That is definitely not an empowering belief.

Can you see how all of that started from your choice of the belief about other people? As you review each of your beliefs and discover those that are limiting or negative, try to see if you can find a more empowering belief to replace it.

Instead of thinking that people are only looking out for number one, I have now adopted the belief that *everyone does the best with what he or she has at every moment in time.* If people attack or hurt me, I choose to believe that they were doing the only thing they could do given their current conditions. Maybe they were blinded by their own pain or limited by their own beliefs, but they were doing the best they were capable of doing. That takes the sting out of things for me. It helps me forgive because I know that I can't ask people to do better than their best in any moment. It is a way for me to let go and move on and that is far more powerful than for me to live in anger and resentment.

Whenever you are facing, a life circumstance that you don't like or want, ask yourself this question, "What belief do I hold that makes me a match to this experience?"

If you look for it, you will find it. Your life experience is always a match to your thoughts, feelings, and beliefs. Look at what you are living and dig a bit deeper to find the beliefs that have created your current situation. Once you find them, you can choose a more positive and empowering belief.

Most people pick up their core beliefs from society, caretakers, friends, family, church, schools, and the media. It's time to stop and think about these beliefs, evaluate their influence in our lives, and choose which ones to keep.

Empowering Beliefs

Here are some samples of empowering beliefs that I've picked up along the way from my teachers, mentors, and coaches. See if any of them ring true for you. If you like them, keep them, use them, and share them. Select the ones you like and write them in your notebook under the tab labeled *Self-Talk*.

- Everything you do and think makes a difference.
- It's never too late to change.
- You can change any situation by changing how you think about it.
- Limits are illusions.
- Your best is always out in front of you.
- When you ask, it is given every single time.
- The past does not have to repeat itself, if you stop focusing on it.
- All your power is in the present moment.
- If you expect a miracle, chances are good you will get one.

- There is always another way.
- I have the ability to make it happen.
- I'm always in the right place at the right time.
- I always get exactly what I need, exactly when I need it.
- I always expect the best.
- Every moment is a new beginning.
- If I think I can, then I CAN!
- Oppression is always self-created.
- Anything is possible, if you can see the possibilities.
- Life is your playground. Go out and give it all you've got.
- What others think of me is none of my business.
- All is well in my world.

We find what we expect to find and
we receive what we ask for.
Albert Hubbard

Chapter 9

Become It!

Who Are You?

Who you are now is a product of the dominant thoughts of your past. The thoughts and beliefs you hold today are the seeds of what you will grow into tomorrow. No matter at what stage you find yourself today, you are always in a perpetual stage of becoming. The best question of all is this, "Who am I becoming?"

How many times have you heard the saying, "You can't teach an old dog new tricks?" That's a false file. It's a bogus thought that keeps you stuck in a cycle of recreating the same thing over and over only because you believe you must. The truth is that you can become whatever you wish.

What Are Your Labels?

Part of the way we identify ourselves is through the labels we use. In earlier chapters you learned that the brain loves to label things. That's how it categorizes and organizes information. It has done the same thing to you! Your brain has given you labels like Wife, Mother, Husband, Father, Grandparent, Child, Daughter, Son—you get the picture. But these identifiers are only the beginning. Your mind attaches labels or descriptors in every category you can imagine.

Not only will it give you a label to describe who you are, but it will attach a value to it as well. Your mind isn't satisfied with the label of golfer, it wants to know how good a golfer you are. You must identify yourself as a pro or amateur and then go so far as to describe your handicap. That way when you announce to the world that you are an amateur "scratch" golfer, we can all be appropriately impressed.

Labels group us together and sometimes separate us from each other. We tend to want to associate with people who are like us, so once we give ourselves a label, we look around for others with the same identity. We join clubs, attend support groups, and become members of organizations that share our self-proclaimed sense of self. Some of these are powerful and positive influences in our lives but others tend to reinforce limiting pictures of who we are and who we can become.

Becoming a Black Belt

My godson Collin had been in karate classes for four years and had been moving through his certification tests with ease. He was now ready to test for his black belt, so of course he invited family and friends to come and watch him. He was certain that this test, like all of the others before, was a formality and that when the day was over we would all be witness to his crowning achievement.

When I arrived at the dojo, I became concerned by what I saw. Collin did not appear to be himself. Instead of the calm confidence he usually displayed, he looked stressed and flustered. His punches and kicks were not the crisp, clean movements I had observed so many times before. I'm no expert, but I could tell he was not performing up to black-belt standards. After the test was completed, the students stood in front of their teacher. I held my breath as one by one, his classmates were called up to receive their black belts. Collin was left standing with one other classmate; both had failed the test.

My heart ached for him. I wondered how he would take it. Would he label himself a failure, hang his head in defeat, and give up his dream? I could see the disappointment in his eyes, but I knew Collin was a fighter. When he focuses on something he has a competitive quality that causes him to stubbornly hold on no matter what happens. After the pain of the moment had passed, I was certain he would bounce back stronger and wiser.

I was right. In the following days, I approached him and told him that if he wanted me to, I would act as his coach and help him prepare mentally for his retest, which was only eight weeks away. He agreed and we immediately went to work on changing the only thing that I knew really mattered—his confidence, self-image, and belief.

During the next eight weeks, we had a lot of fun together. I had him watch inspirational movies like *Miracle on Ice* and *Rocky*. Everything we did together was designed to change his mental picture of himself. One of the assignments I gave him was to watch the movie *Rudy* and to write in his Empowerment Journal the "life lessons" Rudy experienced. I thought he would write about Rudy's tenacity and commitment or perhaps his belief in his dream. Instead, what impressed Collin the most was a statement that had totally escaped me. At one point in the movie, Rudy says to his priest, "God made some people to be football players, and I'm just not one of them." Collin took that statement and rewrote it to become his personal identity declaration: "God made some people to be Black Belt Masters, and **I AM** one of them." What an amazing declaration!

I noticed that once he made that bold claim, he began to change little things that made BIG statements concerning his picture of who he was becoming. He changed his email signature to *Collin Henton, Shotokan Black Belt Master*. He made a vision board for his room with pictures of him in a borrowed black belt so that every morning when he woke up, he would see himself as whom he wanted to become.

Power of I AM Statements

Over the weeks that followed, the transformation in him was incredible. Once he saw himself as a black belt, he increased his workouts at the gym and in the dojo. Because he made the shift in his mind first, his workouts became more fun. He didn't have to use discipline to get to the gym; he was excited and motivated instead. With his vision calling to him and his shift in identity, he had turned something that previously felt like hard work into something he actually looked forward to doing.

I could tell he felt himself changing by the way he carried himself. By the time the testing date rolled around, he knew he was ready. Gone was the strain and tension he had experienced the first time. He had already passed this test in his mind, so this was merely a hoop to jump through. He moved through his kata with poise and completed his sparring with power and confidence. Of course he passed. He had no doubts about it and by then, neither did his Sensei. He claimed his identity and became what he wanted in his mind first, and now he proudly wears his own black belt.

You always know you are proclaiming an identity when you make an I AM statement. What comes after the I AM is the identity you are projecting to the world. Let's look at some of your I AM statements and see if they really represent who you want to become. We are not talking about "telling the truth," we are talking about "telling it like you want it to be." Telling the truth actually reinforces who you currently are. Telling it like you want it to be is the first step in becoming someone or something else. Let's take a few moments and see how you currently describe yourself.

Identifying Your Labels

Part 1 — What identities have you taken on? Go to your workbook and open the section labeled *Self-Talk*. Let's see what statements you are making about yourself. These statements are weaving together an identity that shapes who you are and who you are becoming. List every label you use to describe yourself. You might start with the simple ones like I am a mother. Then move to hobbies, interests, or special skills and talents, like I am a golfer.

Next, include qualities that describe your personality and behavior. These might include things like I am creative, I am lazy, or I am funny. Finally, include other statements that describe the identity you project in the world, like I am an alcoholic, I am a Christian, or I am a survivor.

We all play many roles and therefore, have many identities. Here is the next important step. Let's look at the descriptors you attach to the labels. These are the emotional qualities that really set the tone for how you see yourself.

Part 2 — Go back through the list and add any adjectives that help to fill in the gaps and better define and clarify how you see yourself. Yes, you may use the label of father if you have children; but the real question is what kind of a father are you? There's a lot of difference between an *absent* father and a *loving* father. So go through the list again and write as many I AM statements as you think are appropriate for each label.

Examples:

Daughter – I am an attentive daughter.

Artist – I am a starving artist.

Athlete – I am a fearless athlete.

Slob – I am a fat slob.

Part 3 — Now go through your list one more time and put a plus sign (+) in front of every I AM statement that empowers you. Put a minus sign (–) in front of each one that limits you. Add up the score and see where you stand. Are your predominate identity statements positive or negative?

Here is the exciting part about your identity. YOU get to choose what identity to take on. You will never feel powerful if you hold an identity of a victim. Victims feel helpless and vulnerable so you can't have it both ways. If you want to feel powerful, you have to claim a new identity. It may be that you were victimized at some point in your life, but if you keep telling that story you are literally claiming that identity. You need a new identity to move towards. Like Collin, you must proclaim who you want to become.

So let's do together the activities that Collin used to become a black belt. Describe the person you want to become. What would you look like? How would you feel? What kinds of thoughts would you think? Earlier when we were talking about the power of a vision, I told you that a powerful vision would create a personal identity. We want to create a picture that it is so clear that it pulls you toward it with every breath you take.

Do you remember Sad Susie? Here are some of her I AM statements:

I AM...

never safe.

always being followed.

small and weak.

an easy target.

unlucky with men.

afraid to trust anyone.

As we worked together, I asked Susie what identity she would like to take on. What image would make her feel safe? I asked her to think about her childhood heroines. She decided to use Wonder Woman as her image. She described Wonder Woman's qualities and then made them her own. Whenever she's scared, she asks herself, "What would Wonder Woman do?" and it immediately gives her a picture in her mind of how she wants to behave.

When I asked her to describe her memory of Wonder Woman she said:

Wonder Woman is a strong and beautiful woman. She walks with her head held high. She is proud and confident. She fears no one. She is the protector of others. She is not afraid of her beauty. Everyone loves and trusts her. When she walks into the room, she attracts attention, but it is safe attention. She believes in herself. Other people believe in her too. She goes anywhere she wants because she knows she can handle any situation that comes up. She is attractive enough to have any man she wants.

Next, I asked her to write her new identity statements with I AM qualities that she borrowed from Wonder-Woman. Here is what she wrote.

Just like Wonder Woman, I am a strong and confident woman. I know that I am capable of handling whatever situation arises. I have no reason to live in fear. I know that I can attract the perfect partner into my life. I can live the life I want to live. I am always safe and relaxed.

Can you see that she would attract an entirely different life experience with the second identity? Well, she has. She travels the world with her husband who is an art dealer. Not long ago I bumped into them in the mall, and he was teasing me about what it's like to live with such a strong and independent woman. Standing next to him and holding his arm, she looked up and winked at me. We both knew that she had become strong and independent by design.

Activity 2

Creating Power Statements

Part 1 — Now it's your turn. In your notebook under the *Self-Talk* section, write down as many positive statements as you can think of that describe how you want to view yourself.

Below is a list that I have compiled over the years. If any of them work for you, please take them; if not, maybe they will inspire you as you create your own.

- ✦ I am a creative thinker with brilliant ideas that can change my world.
- ✦ My life is a great demonstration that anything is possible.
- ✦ I have a positive, infectious, optimistic attitude.
- ✦ I am a thriving artist. My work is in ever-increasing demand.
- ✦ I am a rebel always finding my own way.
- ✦ I have an irresistible sense of humor.
- ✦ I love serving others, making their lives better.
- ✦ I radiate love and beauty.
- ✦ I am always in the right place at the right time.
- ✦ I have a brilliant mind.
- ✦ I am a dynamo, full of energy and vitality.
- ✦ I am worthy of all the joy and riches life has to offer.
- ✦ I am bold and courageous.
- ✦ I am happy. I always choose joy and appreciation.
- ✦ I am responsible for all the conditions of my life. I can change anything I am committed to changing.
- ✦ I have an optimistic mind and a fearless heart.
- ✦ I always expect the best, so I always receive the best.
- ✦ I am spontaneous and free.
- ✦ I easily release old patterns, worn-out beliefs, and negative habits of thought.

- My past serves my future. I am free from the past.
- I choose only thoughts and beliefs that serve me.
- All is well, there is nothing to fear.
- I am irresistible, attracting to me exactly the partner I desire.
- Great things always come to me without effort or strain.
- My body knows how to heal itself.
- I am stronger and more vital everyday.
- I love who I am becoming.
- I love and appreciate my powerful body.
- I love my creative mind and superior memory.
- I love making people laugh and feel good.
- I love expressing myself in my own creative ways.
- I love making a difference in the world.
- I am one who is willing to leap.
- I am willing to release resistance, strain, and pain.
- I am willing to take full responsibility for my life.
- I am willing to change.
- I am willing to mentally mind my own business.
- I am willing to be thin and strong.
- I am willing to be wildly successful.
- I am willing to stop sabotaging my own success.
- I am willing to claim my own power and stop listening to the judgments of others.
- I am willing to stop trying to please everyone else.

- ✦ I am in control of my own destiny.
- ✦ I am in control of my choices.
- ✦ I can change anything, because I can choose anything.
- ✦ I am willing to be ME, all of ME, and nothing but ME.

Part 2 — Now read over the list of statements you have written about what you want to believe and experience in your life. If you really claimed this identity, if you really were this kind of person, what would your life be like? Spend a few moments just daydreaming about how your life would be transformed if you took on a new identity—an identity where these statements are not a wish-list but a reality. I'm not asking you to "fake it till you make it," I'm asking you to really feel it. If you can feel it, you can have it. In order to change your identity, to transform into the person you have envisioned, you have to see it, feel it, believe it and you will become it.

> *Take the first step in faith.*
> *You don't have to see the whole staircase.*
> *Just take the first step.*
> Dr. Martin Luther King, Jr.

Chapter 10

Do It!

In my younger days I had a nickname. My friends called me Bam-Bam after the little kid on the Flintstones whose answer to every challenge in life was to use his huge club. That was me. If there were something in my way, no problem, I would just start swinging. BAM! I would knock down a wall if it stood between what I wanted and me. I was a firm believer that more ACTION was always better. I have always been strong in body, mind, and spirit, so I believed that my physical effort could always produce results. It did produce results all right, but not always the ones I wanted. Sometimes I forced massive action when patience would have been more prudent. I can't tell you the number of times in my life I rushed into action, metaphorically smashing down a wall with a wrecking ball, only to find an open window around the corner that would have served me better.

Forcing Versus Asking

What I have come to understand is that having all I want in life is not about forcing, pushing, controlling, or making things happen. It is about asking and allowing things to unfold in perfect timing. It's about letting my desires lead the way and then lining up my thoughts, beliefs, and emotions so that they are all working for me, not against me. It's about holding a vision of what I want and then following the inspiration of Spirit to know when to sit and wait, or when to get up and start swinging.

As I look back over my life, I recognize that there have been many times I was able to create change through discipline and motivation, but the changes were only temporary. That's because motivation comes from outside of us and discipline is forced action, which is rarely permanent. In contrast, there have been times when I saw things come into my life almost effortlessly. Sometimes these changes required action, but when I followed my inspiration to act, life unfolded without pain or strain. The changes I made without struggle seem to stay while those I fought so hard to MAKE HAPPEN were gone as quickly as they came.

That's when I learned the most important secret of all. It's not what you are doing that makes the greatest difference; it's what you are thinking, feeling, and visualizing. I discovered that action taken in fear and frustration usually made matters worse. Creation is about allowing, not about banging things into place. My new personal mantra has become:

My Power Lies in the Flow –
Not in the Go!

Little Bam-Bam still lives in my head and when I hear the advice of my teachers telling me to relax and allow, she screams in my ear, "Okay, how do I DO that?" Then I have to laugh at myself. I see that even when I'm trying to learn how to allow things to flow effortlessly, I am still looking to take action. Old questions still pop into my head: How can I MAKE it happen faster? What are the "to do" items that belong on my list today? What new discipline should I adopt so that I can learn how to let go? Surely there is something I can DO to MAKE IT HAPPEN! Funny, huh?

Let me be clear. I do recognize that sometimes action is required. I'm not belittling the power of action. What I'm doing is trying to help you understand where it lies in the process of change. If you take action first, you will probably be disappointed in the long-term results. If you take time first to discover what you really want, then see it, think it, feel it, and believe it, you will become it. The "doing it" will be the natural next step. You will feel the call of Source. You will hear the voice of God. You will know the pull of Spirit. You will be guided by your passion and in that moment, you won't need discipline to push you into action. When you follow the call from within, you rarely need a big stick.

It is true that we are physical beings and we love to take physical action, so I decided that instead of fighting my natural inclinations, I would try to find a path that satisfied my desire for action and my new understanding of allowing myself to flow—not go. I decided that if I was going to DO something, I should go to work on my habitual negative thoughts. I put on my "to do" list everything that could help me let go and flow.

Going with the Flow – To-Do List

Quiet Time (QT)

Choose a comfortable little corner for yourself, a place where you won't be disturbed. Put on some peaceful music and allow your self to unwind and calm down. This is a time for you to block out any distractions, and to reconnect with your Source. Some people use this opportunity to pray. That's fine, but I urge you to spend the greatest portion of this time listening, breathing, relaxing, and letting go.

Meditation is a powerful tool to quiet your negative, worrying, problem-solving mind. This is your time to let go of your thoughts and just be still. Taking a break from your busy day to release the resistant energy in your body can make all the difference in learning the art of allowing instead of the discipline of doing.

Be still and focus on your breath. Allow your mind to let go. You can use a guided meditation, which will also give you the benefit of reducing stress. If you don't like the idea of listening to someone else's voice, you can listen to peaceful music while you focus on something simple like your breathing, a small desktop fountain, or even a candle. Make sure you have a few minutes every day to quiet your mind, release, and let go.

Mini Movies

Mini movies are short picture shows you see in your mind to help you visualize yourself living your dreams. My high school softball coach was the first to teach me the power of mental imagery. Every day, at the end of practice, she asked us to lie down on the grass and do our stretching routine. During that time, she would give us a game situation and ask us to imagine ourselves executing the perfect play. My favorite was the one she called our *Hero Movie*. She said, "Okay, girls, imagine that we are up by one run in the bottom of the 7th inning in the state championship game. Our opponent is batting. The bases are loaded with only one out. The ball is hit to you, and you execute the perfect, defensive double-play to win the game." Obviously, each of us had different pictures in our minds depending on the position we played. I was the third baseman.

I imagined that the runner on third was leading off the bag. When the batter hit a line drive, I caught the ball and, in one fluid motion, tagged the lead runner who was trying to get back to third. I played it in my mind over and over and felt the feelings of being lifted onto the shoulders of my teammates and carried around the field as we won the state trophy.

As "luck" would have it, we were playing in a quarterfinal game on a rainy Saturday afternoon. The field was sloppy, but the tournament director needed to get our game completed, so we took the field. In the 5th inning our opponents started to gain some momentum, and we found ourselves deep in a hole. They had runners on first and third with no outs. The runner on third was acting a bit antsy, and I knew she was going to try to run so I stayed closer to the baseline than usual.

Just then, the batter hit a line drive right between the base and me. At that moment, everything seemed to shift into slow motion as

I dove to my right reaching for the ball. I felt it hit my glove seconds before I landed face-first in a mud puddle. I'd caught the ball and even though I couldn't see, I knew the runner was off the base. Without looking, I turned and lunged toward her as she scrambled to get back to the base. After tackling her, I leaped to my feet and rocketed the ball to first catching that runner off the bag as well.

I stood stunned as my teammates rushed over to congratulate me. That's when it hit me; I had just pulled off a triple play that was even better than my mental imagery. I had practiced that play so many times in my head that when the time was right, my body just delivered what my mind had seen and felt as real. I attracted the circumstances and events to make my visualization become my reality. When the celebration was over, my coach came over to me and said, "I've never seen you move so fast." She winked at me, and I knew that she knew, it was our *Hero Movie* that had made it possible.

That experience made me a believer in the power of mental mini movies. You, too, can gain confidence in the power of this process, which can bring to you all the desires of your heart. You need to start with something easy, fun, and lighthearted so that resistance and doubt won't be working against you. Use your notebook to write out these pictures, if that helps you get focused. Then close your eyes and let your mind run loose. When you were a kid, your teachers told you to get your head out of the clouds, but I'm telling you to get back up there. Daydreaming, imagining, and visualizing are great tools for your personal empowerment.

Imagination is more important than knowledge.
Albert Einstein

Power Statements

You are constantly affirming who you are and what you expect from life with every thought, word, and deed. Now let's think about what that means. Do you remember the exercises we have been doing to identify your habitual thoughts, beliefs, and feelings? Each of those acts is an affirmation. Your affirmations send out signals in the world that act like little magnets attracting matching experiences back to you.

Here is an everyday example. You wake up a bit grumpy and think to yourself, "I hate Mondays." As you get out of bed, you stub your toe on the corner of the bed and think to yourself, "I should have stayed in bed and called in sick." In your disconnected state, you spill your coffee on your shirt and have to take time to change. Your frustration builds as you think to yourself, "I knew I shouldn't have gotten up. Now I'm going to be late!" As you take the entrance ramp to the freeway, you are greeted with a traffic jam as far as you can see. At that moment your cell phone rings; it's your boss. From the tone in his voice, you can tell you are already in trouble. Before you know it, you have a splitting headache. As you pop a few pills, you remember your morning affirmation: I should have stayed in bed and called in sick.

So, how do you change the moment-to-moment self-talk that acts like affirmations in your life? You must become conscious of the thoughts you think and the statements you make. If the conscious affirmations you are already making aren't empowering you, you can choose new ones. There are outstanding books available that have hundreds of affirmations you can pick and choose from. Remember that you are selecting new positive Power Statements.

When you first start using them, they won't feel natural, so sometimes your mind will want to discount them. If you are in debt up to your ears and you choose a new affirmation such as, "I am living an abundant life," your brain will challenge that new statement since it doesn't match your habitual belief, "I'll never get ahead." Don't let that discourage you. Remind yourself that you are making changes and these new thoughts will lead the way to new habitual thinking patterns which will then lead to new life experiences.

Use the *Self-Talk* section of your notebook to collect affirmations and positive statements. I head each page of my notebook with a different topic and whenever I read a great statement or hear someone else use a positive proclamation, I capture it on that page. Every morning at the end of my QT, I read over my Power Statements. It always makes me feel fantastic.

Quick guidelines for writing your own Power Statements:

- Always write them in the present: I have, I am—instead of I want, or I will someday have.

- Always affirm in the positive: I am calm and poised—instead of I'm not going to be afraid any more.

- Keep them short and sweet: I am getting stronger with every breath I take. Not a two-page dissertation. The difference is that the two-page dissertation is probably a great vision statement, but affirmations are short, general thoughts that race through your mind in a heartbeat.

- See the Alpha Affirmations segment in the Tools chapter for more on how and when to use your affirmations.

Give your mind some new Power Statements to repeat and you will quickly see your dominant thoughts and feelings beginning to swing to the positive and powerful side of the continuum.

Joy Journal

One of the most powerful energies available to you is joy. Call it bliss, happiness, appreciation, pleasure, gratitude, or even thankfulness; it's the most powerful energy on earth. When you focus on things that make you happy and feel the emotion of gratitude for those things in your life, then you are really moving in the right direction.

My favorite movie as a kid was the musical *The Sound of Music*. I loved the scene where Maria is singing to the frightened Von Trapp children during a thunderstorm. The song goes like this: "When the dog bites, when the bee stings, when I'm feeling sad, I simply remember my favorite things, and then I don't feel so bad."

Let's find out what some of your favorite things are. Start by picking anything in your life that makes you smile. Focus on memories that warm your heart, and think back over the times that have caused you to laugh. Look around your current environment for things that are a delight to your senses. What little things in your life bring you joy? What's working in your life? What do you treasure? The answers to all these questions are things to capture in your *Joy Journal* every day.

When you read accounts of people who report having "near death experiences," they always say they were changed by the event. They claim to have a heightened state of appreciation for every new day. They seem to live life from a new perspective as though each moment is a cherished gift. What a tremendous difference from the way many people live. Do you live your life in a constant state of appreciation for another day to romp and play, or are you one of the people that Henry David Thoreau wrote about when he said, "Most men live lives of quiet desperation."

If you will look for what makes you happy and you appreciate all the gifts you have in your life, I promise that, just like the Von Trapp children, even when the bee stings, you won't feel so bad.

"When you appreciate the little things,
the big things will find you irresistible."
Melinda Mercedes Balling

Action

Action means you set things into motion. It is the moment when you take a leap of faith, follow your passion, listen to your inspiration, and put your spirit into motion. It is that moment when you take the next logical step.

When I was standing at the front of the fire lines on the closing night of the Tony Robbins seminar, there was a moment when I knew I had to take action or I would not make it across the fire. I waited until the moment when I felt the call of inspiration. I worked on my thoughts and beliefs and once they were in the right place, I felt the pull of my vision; I heard that still small voice within saying, "Now!" and I walked with confidence. No struggle, no pain and yet, I most definitely experienced gain.

I believe that words are very limited in their ability to truly teach, but personal experience can teach in a heartbeat. That's why I often conclude my live seminars with a board-break activity. I love the board-break because it is a physical demonstration of breaking through mental limits. It is an opportunity for my participants to try out the new strategies they have learned. I have walked more than a hundred thousand people, ages 10 – 86, through this experience and it never fails to amaze me. The board is a great metaphor for all the other moments in their lives when they will face an obstacle that looks impossible, but in truth that obstacle is nothing but an illusion. It is a perfect example of how the transformational tools I've shared with you in this book actually work.

First, you must want to do it. If you don't, you'll never be successful. Next you have to see it, believe it, feel it, and finally when all those steps are in place, you have to do it. You have to swing, or the board is **not** going to break. Sometimes, when I work with youth groups, I get kids who just want to ignore the steps and start swinging. (Sounds a lot like BAM-BAM.) Inevitably, all they do is get a sore hand and decide that they CAN'T do it. I love it when that happens because then I really have their attention.

To break a board, it's easiest if you get your mind, body, and soul all lined up together. Once these three identities become aligned, you can go right through the board without struggle or pain.

That moment is one of my favorites. When I am holding the board for a young woman, it's like having a front row seat to watch the amazing transformation that occurs when she summons up the courage to claim her vision. One minute I see a fearful expression in her eyes. The instant her hand breaks through the board, there is a split second of disbelief. Then her eyes widen and a glowing smile spreads across her face.

Sometimes there are screams and sometimes there are tears as energy rushes through their bodies. Then there is a celebration of accomplishment—cheering, dancing, and clapping the broken board pieces together. All of it creates that "ah-ha" moment that teaches what words can't. You CAN do anything your heart desires if you want it, see it, think it, feel it, believe it, become it and when the moment is right, do it.

I want to give you a moment like that right now. Since I'm not sitting with you, I can't coach you through a board-break, but I can coach you through the steps to help you feel the same sense of accomplishment. Open your notebook and let's get started.

Let It Go and Flow

Part 1 — **Choosing a Project.** In your notebook, go to the activities from Chapter 4 and review your lists: To Do, To Be, To Have and To Give. Find something on the list that you have always wanted to experience, something that you can become excited about, and we will use that as our focus for this activity.

Part 2 — **Writing Your Negative Chatter.** Now as you look at this "thing" that you have always wanted to do, be, have, or give, let me ask you an important question: If it is so important to you, why haven't you done it yet? Take a few moments now to list all the excuses you have used throughout the years to hold yourself apart from this important goal.

First, let me show you all the negative chatter I had to overcome to accomplish one of my dreams—writing this book. I have been talking about writing it for more than 20 years and I even started it a few times, but each time I got terrified and quit. Here is a peek inside my old limiting thinking patterns. After you read the example, go to your notebook and write your story.

> *"First of all, Erickson, you can't write a self-help book until you 'have it all together.' If your life isn't perfect in every way, then no one's going to take you seriously. Besides, who do you think you are? You're no Tony Robbins, that's for sure. And, what about the FACT that you can't spell? Where are you going to find an editor who can help you to communicate your message? Even if you could find someone to help, where are you going to find the time to write since you're on the road speaking so much? And if you did manage to get it written, how would you find a publisher to print and distribute it? You're nobody! What publisher wants to take a chance on a no-name, first-time author? If you can't get a publisher, you would have to print it yourself and where would you get the money to do that? And what if you go to all that trouble and no one likes your book?"*

Part 3 — **Changing Your Story**. Look at your negative chatter; can you see why it hasn't happened yet? Now it's time to do something about it. Remember, ***your power lies in the flow—not in the go!*** So let's get you into the flow. Do each of the **Go with the Flow Items** listed below.

Mini Movie – Write out your mini movie as though you are the screenwriter, producer, editor, actor, and viewer. See yourself in your own movie. Write it exactly as you want to experience it. Remember to include all the sensory rich information you can imagine. Then, every morning watch the movie in your imagination.

Power Statement – Write out your statements, so that as you recite them, they become your new thought affirmations. As you read them, they should help you feel as though you already possess this item or are living this experience.

Joy Journal – You can write in your *Joy Journal* in the morning or at night. The advantage of writing in the morning is that it starts your day off in an attitude of gratitude. The advantage of writing at night is that you drift off to sleep having mentally reviewed your day, capturing every little moment to appreciate in your journal. Either way, your *Joy Journal* is helping you look for things that make you smile.

QT – Find a quiet place where you can sit for a few moments every day and just be still. Before you leave your QT, review your Mini Movie and your Power Statements. I like doing this in the morning because it sets the tone for the day.

Now DO IT!

Practice the activities in part three, over and over every day, as many times a day as you can. Then listen for inspiration to ACT! You will know when that time comes. Just like the impulse to yawn can't be denied, neither can your impulse to take action when the timing is right. When it comes, follow your instinct and commit 100%. Pour your whole heart and soul into it, and you will watch your dreams unfold with amazing ease.

> *God speaks to us everyday,*
> *only we don't know how to listen.*
> Mahatma Gandhi

Chapter 11

Transform It!

By now you know that every thought you think and every word you speak is actually an affirmation that has transformational power. It's true that your words help to create your reality, but so does everything you think, do, and feel every waking moment of your life. It all counts, because it is all creative energy.

If you want your life to be different, you must change. You must transform your emotions, outlook, thoughts, words, core programming, and conscious mindset. The good news is that it is easier than you might think. The key is inundating your mind with new programming to help it release its grip on the old. Bombarding the conscious and subconscious mind takes some time but you will begin to feel the change almost immediately.

Power Steps to Bombard Your Mind

#1. Get Conscious

First, you must be conscious of your current programming. The vast majority of humanity walks around unconsciously incompetent. That means they have no idea what's truly going on in their life and as a result, they can't figure out how to make things work. When someone is unconsciously incompetent, they feel powerless and are likely to look for others to blame because it explains why they are stuck. You might hear them blaming the government, the president, their company, their parents, their genes, their history, their children, their former spouse, and so on for all of the problems in their lives. But, blaming anything or anyone for the circumstances of your life causes you to give up your power. Once you give up your power, you give up the ability to make true change.

#2. Take Responsibility for Your Life

Years ago, when I was at my heaviest weight, my therapist told me to stand in front of the mirror and say, "Woo-hoo, look what I did! Look how successful I was at creating this massive body!" Now at first glance that may seem strange, but the first time I did it, I felt free. By claiming responsibility for the condition that I had already created, I gave myself the power to believe I could create something different. There is such power in taking responsibility for your own creations, and that can only happen, if you first become conscious.

#3. Get Competent

You can master anything in life if you find the right tools, get the best training, work with an expert trainer or coach, and commit to practice a new skill until you perfect it. Can you feel the sense of power that comes with knowing you can gain any skill, if you are committed to do whatever it takes? Don't be discouraged, if you're not exactly where you want to be right now. Just find the support you need and commit to the process.

#4. Use the Right Tools

My grandpa used to say to me, "Debbie, you can do anything if you use the right tool for the job." I've always considered that profound advice. If you wanted to dig a hole for a new swimming pool in your backyard and someone handed you a spoon, you would see that the job would take a long time. You might go out into the yard and start digging with passion and a great attitude, but in a very short amount of time you would become discouraged. The question is, what follows the discouragement? Do you give up and say, "I just can't do this. It's taking too long! I'm just not a good digger." Or would you simply say, "This is a poor strategy, I need a better tool."

Transforming your mind is very similar. If you understand neuroscience, you can choose appropriate tools to create the shifts you are looking for. Mastering these tools takes time, but the results can be spectacular. My advice to you is to never question your innate ability, only your strategy.

#5. Repetition is the Key to Mastery

From birth to age seven, the human mind is completely moldable, ready to absorb any information that comes its way. Unfortunately by their 17th birthday, the average child in America has heard negative messages about their abilities approximately 150,000 times. In contrast, they have heard positive reinforcement about 5,000 times. That means, as children, we are programmed 30 to 1 with more negative feedback about our potential than positive. To make matters worse, our brains are wired to hold on to the negative more than positive as a survival mechanism. As a result of childhood experiences, most humans spend the vast majority of their lives in fear and doubt instead of excitement and confidence.

In addition, new research shows that we need about 10,000 repetitions to own a new habit, so you can see that most of us never got enough positive reinforcement to even reach that level. No wonder there is so much fear and frustration in the world.

Your job is to search for the positive. You have to want to see the good and be willing to look for the gift in every life situation. If you seek – you will find, but the seeking must be intentional. You rarely stumble upon a great attitude. You must choose it everyday. You have to repeat, repeat, and repeat again in order to master any new skill, belief, attitude, and therefore outcome.

The Process of Transformation

Transformation is life changing for a reason. You start with one form and move to another. That means there is no going back to the original condition. Your life is forever changed because awareness means you see everything from a new perspective. You can never feel helpless again because you know you have the power to choose your thoughts. You know you have the power to shift your emotions and therefore the ability to create a different life experience. When you know how things work and you have transformational tools, you always have the power to choose a new path.

I love the story of the transformation of the caterpillar to the butterfly, because it describes so beautifully the process of change. The caterpillar creates a safe place to begin its change by spinning a cocoon. This structure carefully supports the caterpillar throughout the process. When the butterfly is ready to break free, it extends its wings, pushing, unfolding, and flapping them so that they can break through the wall of the cocoon. The act of pushing through the limit of the cocoon actually fills the wings with fluid that is needed for the butterfly to fly and be free.

So it is with us. We need a safe environment to move through this process. We need a safe place to play, learn new tools, examine our lives, expand our comfort zone, try on our new identity, heal our past, and step into our greatness. From that safe place, we expand and push through the limits that have held us captive. We free ourselves to be the powerful individuals we were born to be.

I created *RutBusting for Women* for that purpose. It provides a safe community to learn and grow, a place to gain the transformational tools you need to continue your journey. It's a place to practice your skills and step into your power with ease, grace, and love. You will see butterflies all over my website and throughout my programs. They are a constant reminder that changing our lives is a natural process and a symbol of our constant becoming.

> *"Every life experience has value if you learn to make your past serve your future."*
> Deb Erickson

Your Life Timeline

Let's see how we can make your past serve your future. We can do that by creating a timeline of your life and looking for the gifts that your past will inevitably provide.

Step 1. Create a Timeline

Review some of your major life memories. You can break them down by decades, categories, life phases, or any other way that makes sense to you. On a piece of paper, list significant memories that caused strong emotions. Include those that you believe played a part in shaping who you have become.

On a different sheet of paper, divide the page into three vertical columns. At the top of the first column write "My Memory". At the top of the second write "Current Impact", and at the top of the third column write "The Gift".

As you look through the memories you listed, choose one to write in the first column. In the second column, describe the impact this experience had on your life.

My Memory	Current Impact	The Gift

Here is a sample memory shared by a client I will call Barbara:

Memory:

Barbara has very few memories of her childhood, but one remains very vivid. She remembers an incident in high school when she showed up to her first dance. Her family was quite poor and being the last of seven children, she was always dressed in her older sister's hand-me-downs. Her clothes were always well worn and out of style, but on this occasion, her mother had shopped at the local thrift store for something "new". Barbara showed up expecting to finally fit in with the cool girls. However, when she walked into the dance, she was met by laughter and ridicule instead. Sally, the head cheerleader, walked up to her and in a cruel tone said, "So, you think wearing my leftovers makes you cool? Not even close. You are not woman enough to wear my old dress." Saying that she grabbed the dress and ripped the lace right off. Barbara stood in the middle of the dance with her dress ripped to shreds and everyone laughing at her.

How has this memory impacted her life?

To this day, Barbara feels like she doesn't fit in. She is obsessive about how she looks, what she wears, and how people look at her. If she is in public and people are laughing across the room, she assumes it is about her. She has spent a fortune shopping for the latest fashions, but she always feels ugly. She has been married four times and has left each marriage because she didn't feel like she was appreciated and loved enough. She is a compulsive people pleaser, doing anything that is required to gain the approval of others.

Remember, this is just one memory and one way her life has been shaped. The power of this activity is to recover as many memories as you can. Then evaluate all the ways the experience has shaped your current reality. The memories can be a specific moment in time, or they can be an environment-based memory such as:

- There was never any money for things I wanted.
- My dad was always drunk and I had to tiptoe around to keep him from going into a rage.

- My mom was always sad and withdrawn. I don't ever remember her holding me and telling me she loved me.
- No matter how hard I tried, my brother was always the favorite. Nothing I did was ever right.
- No one ever listened to me. I felt invisible.

Let your mind run through your life experiences and capture anything you think is significant. Write them all down and ask yourself how each has influenced your life.

Step 2. The Gift

As you review the columns can you see how, just like Barbara, your current reality has been shaped by your early experiences? The good news is that you can redefine the meaning of anything in your past. We are going to go back and review each memory and ask the question, "What is the gift that was hiding behind this experience?"

When I asked Barbara to review her story, she decided that the gift was that she realized how she had given up her power by letting a few high school girls define her worth. She saw how one event had put her on a path of desperately chasing approval in every aspect of her life. She faced the fact that she would never gain the approval she was looking for from other people. She decided to give herself approval. She decided that loving herself was all she needed.

Within six months, Barbara turned her life around. She is now successful in her own eyes, is happier with how she looks, is repairing her marriage, feels more alive than ever, and is developing a thriving business all because she was willing to look at the gift of her past instead of the pain.

What gifts is your past waiting to give you? Spend some time, claim the gifts, and transform your life.

> *"No one can make you feel inferior without your consent."*
> Eleanor Roosevelt

Chapter 12

Putting It All Together

We have covered a lot of ground together and, if you have been doing the activities throughout the book, you have deepened your understanding of the role your mind plays in the process of creating your life experience. By now you have also observed the power of attraction, in action, in a very personal way. I hope you have gotten plenty of practice expressing your appreciation in your Joy Journal, creating and playing your own mental Mini Movies, and using Power Statements to shape your future reality. You should also have a clear picture of how to use the eight steps for getting out of your mental and emotional ruts. So now, it is time to get on with your life.

Making a Total Commitment

First, let me tell you that in order to achieve your dreams, you must commit everything you have—your whole mind, heart, body, and spirit. When you give everything you have, you send out into the world, an energy that shouts, "I will not be denied!" That enthusiasm and determination will take you there. That commitment is an irresistible force that will bring to you the desires of your heart—to have what you want to have, to become who you intend to be, to do what your heart inspires you to do, and to contribute to the world what you are called to contribute. All great teachers, throughout the ages, have advised their students to expect success. What you expect is what you will get, so let's talk about a few challenges you will face as you get on with your life.

Eliminating Failure Files

First of all, there is no such thing as failure. It is a cruel, coldhearted concept that some negative mind fabricated and it has been passed on generation after generation. A continued thought pattern of failure will rob you of your potential and steal your dreams. It's a false file, a bogus belief that is masquerading as truth. It is nothing more than the result of looking through those dirty glasses and coming to an erroneous conclusion. However, that conclusion has the power to control your life if you let it.

Here is a different, more positive definition. This one concept can change your life forever: Failure is merely a setback, a delay, and a temporary obstruction. It is life's message that "There's a better way."

Here's how I view failure:

- It means that you should try something else.
- It's a reminder to look for a window instead of trying to knock down a wall.
- It means that there is a new opportunity that awaits you around the corner.
- It means that you should look for a new strategy or acquire more training.
- It means that things are not properly aligned and ready yet. You need to wait patiently. Sometimes our impatience causes us to label as failure, something that wasn't quite ready to be plucked.

Life is a process, a journey that takes you toward your dreams. That suggests that sometimes you move forward, sometimes you move back, and sometimes you sit and wait for inspiration. When you are ready, you take a step and review the feedback. You evaluate your results, see if you need to make any course corrections, and when you feel inspired, you take another step.

Sometimes the call of Source is so strong that you will throw caution to the wind and race towards it. Sometimes you will sit in sweet silence rejuvenating, regrouping, and realigning your thoughts. Sometimes you may feel lost as though you are wandering in the wilderness. It's okay; it's all part of the journey.

Remember that you can always get where you want to go from wherever you find yourself by using your EGS—Emotional Guidance System. So ask for direction, listen for that still small voice, feel your spirit's guidance, and then move. All that you desire awaits you. Don't let a phony file labeled *Failure* cloud your vision or hold you apart from living the life of your dreams.

Transforming Fear into Courage

Fear, just like failure, is nothing more than the brain's label for a specific set of physical sensations. That's it. You feel something and your brain calls it fear.

Have you ever watched people on a rollercoaster? Their eyes are wide open, their hair is standing straight up, and they're screaming their lungs out. You can't tell which ones are truly terrified and which ones are genuinely thrilled with the ride.

Suppose that you are on that rollercoaster. Here's what is happening in your body. The brain opens a file. Inside are warnings that the brain perceives as a threat to its survival, and it releases adrenaline into your system to give you everything you need to handle the situation. Some people hate the feeling and label it fear. Others are thrilled by it and call it excitement. Some define their increased heart rate as panic; others get a rush from it. It's all about how you respond and define your experience.

If you can redefine fear, you can make it your friend instead of your enemy. Close your eyes for a moment and think about doing something that in the past has caused you great fear. Maybe it's speaking in public, cold calling a new prospect, or asking your boss for a raise. Whatever it is, I want you to think about it right now. Can you feel the physical sensations you call fear? Good.

Now let's find a new label for that file. When you feel your heart race and those butterflies in your stomach, instead of calling that physical sensation fear, call it God Power. Call it the power of the universe flooding through your body, or even the arrival of your angels or angel being presenting itself to support you. Call it whatever you like, but choose to rename the file something powerful and positive and you will make fear your friend.

Remember that your brain wants to stay comfortably in a rut. Like a child who feels secure with the same routine, your adult mind also likes habits and schedules. So, when you decide you are going to change your negative thinking habits, your mind will rebel. The more you stretch yourself, the more fear you will face. Most people let that fear stop them. Fear can be powerfully persuasive and, if you let it, it will stop you from pursuing your dream. Instead, choose today to transform your fear into courage and you will never be stopped by fear again.

Having Fun

More than anything else, you must lighten up and have fun. When you are present and loving life, you flow. When you are struggling or trying to force something to happen, you tend to tense up. Do you remember taking swimming lessons and learning to float? You soon discovered that when you fight and struggle, you sink right to the bottom. When you relax and let go, floating is natural and easy. So, relax and have fun; make the world your playground. Let go and your inner strength and genius will emerge. Your passion will flow, and you will go places you may not yet have dreamed possible.

In 1992, Maryanne Williamson wrote a book entitled "A Return to Love" which fell into the hands of Nelson Mandela, the South African civil rights leader who became known as the most famous prisoner in the world. In his 1994 Inaugural Address, he quoted from Williamson's book. See if it inspires you as it did Mandela after spending 30 years in prison.

Our deepest fear is not that we are inadequate.
Our deepest fear is that we are powerful
beyond measure. It is our light, not our darkness,
that frightens us most. We ask ourselves,
"Who am I to be brilliant, gorgeous, talented,
and famous?" Actually, who are you not to be?
You are a child of God.
Your playing small does not serve the world.
There is nothing enlightened about shrinking so
that people won't feel insecure around you.
We were born to make manifest the glory of God
that is within us. It's not just in some of us, it's in
all of us. And when we let our own light shine, we
unconsciously give other people permission to do
the same. As we are liberated from our own fear,
our presence automatically liberates others.

Maryanne Williamson

From My Heart to Yours

All the bounties of life await you. You have nothing to fear. Be strong and courageous. Be yourself. You are growing and becoming better every day. Embrace your emotions. Commit to play the game with your entire being. Have faith that you have been given the abilities and opportunities to live your dreams. Believe in the promise that when you ask it is given. Know that you are an amazing creation. Now it's time to…

Get Out of the Rut,
and On With Your Life.

Who is Deb Erickson?

After graduating from Illinois State University in 1978, Deb spent the first 10 years of her professional career as a teacher and athletic coach, winning awards for her achievements in the classroom and on the court. As a student learning principles of success, Deb challenged herself by moving into the business arena where she excelled as a sales trainer and team manager for companies like The Equitable, The American Heart Association, and The University of Phoenix.

Deb continued her education, studying breakthroughs in neuroscience while working towards her Masters Degree in Counseling. Driven to expand her reach, she pursued her life's dream to become an inspirational speaker and empowerment coach. That dream was the driving force behind creating her own personal and professional development company, ICAN Institute, Inc.

Over the last 20 years, Deb has gained international acclaim as a speaker, radio personality, author, and transformational coach. While her client list is a who's who of Fortune 500 companies, Deb's greatest passion has been mastering the art of coaching women to step into their greatness through her live events and online programs.

Her newest programs, RutBusting for Women and ICAN Coach teach brain-training techniques that create significant change quickly with lasting results. Her new CD, Embracing Change, is the first in her Alpha Transformational Systems for Women series. These audio recordings are having an impact on women who are hungry to move past personal obstacles and into their own power.

empowering women to step into their greatness!

www.deberickson.com